THE WHOLE-BRAIN SOLUTION

Thinking tools to help students observe, make connections, and solve problems

TRICIA ARMSTRONG

Pembroke Publishers Limited

Dedicated to the librarians and library clerks of Canmore, Alberta — wonderful wilderness women who are always willing to share information. Thank you all.

© 2003 Pembroke Publishers
538 Hood Road
Markham, Ontario, Canada L3R 3K9
www.pembrokepublishers.com

Distributed in the U.S. by Stenhouse Publishers
477 Congress Street
Portland, ME 04101
www.stenhouse.com

We acknowledge the financial support of the Government of Canada through the Book Publishing Industry Development Program (BPIDP) for our publishing activities.

We acknowledge the Government of Ontario through the Ontario Media Development Corporation's Ontario Book Initiative.

National Library of Canada Cataloguing in Publication

Armstrong, Tricia,
   The whole-brain solution : thinking tools to help students observe, make connections and solve problems / Tricia Armstrong.

Includes bibliographical references and index.
For use in grades 6–10.
ISBN 1-55138-156-7

   1. Critical thinking—Study and teaching 2. Problem solving—Study and teaching I. Title.

LB1590.3.A73 2003   370.15'   C2003-902742-2

Editor: Carol-Ann Freeman
Cover Design: John Zehethofer
Cover Photography: Ajay Photographics
Typesetting: Jay Tee Graphics Ltd.

Printed and bound in Canada
9 8 7 6 5 4 3 2 1

Contents

Introduction

Welcome to *The Whole-Brain Solution*, a collection of higher-order thinking tools for enlivening students' receptivity, deepening their understanding, and increasing their ability to connect knowledge to their own lives. What is the whole-brain solution? The answer lies in the functions of the two hemispheres of the brain. The left hemisphere specializes in tasks that require logic and language, and tends to be used more by writers, scientists, and mathematicians. The right hemisphere deals with pattern recognition and creativity, and tends to be used more by artists, musicians, and inventors. The creative thinking tools in *The Whole-Brain Solution* help to unify the functions of right and left hemispheres, strengthening and integrating both the sequential and simultaneous processes of thought.

What are higher-order thinking tools?

Higher-order thinking tools are strategies that increase students' participation in the learning process through identifying relevance, engaging transformational skills, and actively using information. These strategies allow for many different results, and encourage open-ended discussion, questioning, and investigating. By contrast, lower-order mental tasks, such as remembering and recalling, are based on storage and retrieval of information and often require a single correct answer. Broadly speaking, some higher-order thinking strategies, such as analyzing, evaluating, and identifying, are "deconstructing" tools and are termed critical thinking. Strategies such as synthesizing, connecting, and transforming, are "constructing" tools and are termed creative thinking. These two types of tools are not completely separate categories, and they are often found working together within the same activity.

How do higher-order thinking tools help to raise students' achievement levels?

Higher-order thinking tools are not about *what* to think, they are about *how* to think. Consider a student's current standing on a rubric level. In order to rise to a higher level of achievement, the student needs to take the concepts, skills, or processes to a deeper level, in other words to more fully "own" the knowledge. When higher-order thinking tools are engaged, a student's interest and involvement in the information increase, and there are more "Now I see!" moments, more insights into the purpose of the information and the benefits of applying it. In other words, the student's participation in and appreciation of the relevance of learning are heightened and, as a result, achievement and satisfaction in learning increase.

Wouldn't students get better grades if they focused their time and energy on remembering and recalling rather than on developing higher-order thinking tools?

If education was only a process of memorizing and recalling, higher-order thinking tools might be limited in their use to developing more creative ways to memorize and recall (in fact Chapter 1 includes several strategies for recalling information). However, education is a process of preparing students to be successful, productive members of society, and the more opportunities students have to understand and integrate the information they are accumulating, the better they can use it to solve problems and make decisions. And if a goal of education is to develop citizens who will contribute directly to the progress and happiness of civilization as a whole, then the need for creativity becomes even greater.

Which higher-order thinking tools are featured in this book?

Each chapter in *The Whole-Brain Solution* focuses on developing a thinking tool and a related skill.

Thinking Tools	Related Skills
1. Observing	Visualizing
2. Generating ideas	Abstracting
3. Asking questions	Hypothesizing
4. Connecting	Mapping
5. Making analogies	Naming
6. Recognizing patterns	Making patterns
7. Solving problems	Making decisions
8. Transforming	Making models
9. Synthesizing	Empathizing

1. Observing

Observations are facts learned directly through the senses. Students can improve their ability to observe from a variety of perspectives, and to visualize and recall with increased clarity. Careful observation is an important skill for artists, scientists, naturalists, doctors, actors, and writers. The related skill of **visualizing** helps students form an image of what they are learning about, recall things visually, and imagine how they might look in the future.

2. Generating ideas

Generating ideas involves focusing attention, enlivening prior knowledge, and inspiring new thoughts. The process of generation calls for divergent thinking, which involves originality, a search for information, and novel answers. The strategies in this chapter can help students stimulate creativity by breaking up predictable thinking patterns and inspiring a wider range of possibilities. Skills in generating ideas are especially important in business, the fine arts, design, city planning, government, and problem solving. The related skill of **abstracting** helps students reduce complicated things to simple principles.

3. Asking questions

Asking questions is an important part of learning because it increases alertness and helps to connect information with prior knowledge and experience.

Students can practise refining and focusing their questions so that they better identify what they would like to know and elicit more useful information. Skill in questioning is important in the fields of research, medicine, counseling, police work, marketing, and design. The related skill of **hypothesizing** helps students to suggest possible solutions to a question based on present knowledge and experience.

4. Connecting

The ability to see and make connections lies at the heart of creative and innovative thinking. Students can broaden their appreciation of the interconnectedness and interrelatedness of life by finding links among objects, ideas, and processes. Finding similarities among differences helps students to make and appreciate new combinations. Teachers, philosophers, artists, inventors, medical researchers, counselors, and architects call upon their connecting skills in everyday life. The related skill of **mapping** helps students to see connections through graphically representing a topic, issue, or subject.

5. Making analogies

An analogy is a comparison between two dissimilar objects, ideas, or processes that have some qualities in common. Often, analogies explain the unfamiliar by using the familiar, such as when a camera is compared to an eye. Analogies are an essential part of creativity because they provide the conceptual basis for theories and ideas by identifying relationships between things that cannot be explicitly compared or literally equated. Students can expand their thinking by using analogies to find and consider relationships. Poets, visual artists, inventors, scientists, mathematicians, and humorists make regular use of analogies in their work. The related skill of **naming** helps students to notice details in appearance, function, location, and so on.

6. Recognizing patterns

Recognizing patterns is the process of identifying the interrelationship of parts in a whole. It involves finding an arrangement of qualities, form, style, shapes, colors, design, etc. Students can improve their ability to identify and work with patterns by focusing on central features and understanding connections within a system. Pattern skills are important scientific and artistic tools and are used extensively in medicine, engineering, dance, music, art, math, and languages. Students can manifest pattern skills by **making patterns**, which helps them to see how parts fit together to form coherent wholes.

7. Solving problems

Defining a problem is a large part of solving a problem, whether it is a scientific investigation or a day-to-day decision. Solving a problem includes working through a process to identify possible solutions and selecting the best one. Students can strengthen their ability to approach a problem in an organized way by working with a variety of problem-solving techniques and applying them to different situations. Problem-solving skills are called upon in every walk of life, especially in management, the legal professions, counseling, police work, city planning, engineering, architecture, and medicine. The related skill of **making decisions** helps students to understand the needs of the various parts of a situation and choose appropriate action from a range of possibilities.

8. Transforming

Transforming is the process of internalizing information and then presenting it in a different way. The transforming process incorporates two or more thinking tools serially (such as observing and abstracting, or naming, visualizing, and connecting). Students can use transforming skills to think dimensionally (e.g., estimating, visualizing geometric shapes), to make knowledge relevant, and to communicate their knowledge to others through a variety of formats. Transforming is especially useful in teaching, engineering, designing, architecture, computing science, medicine, visual arts, and mathematics. The related skill of **making models** helps students to create a mental image or physical representation to explain an object, event, or process.

9. Synthesizing

Synthesizing is the process of putting together parts to form wholes. It involves a simultaneous integration of many higher-order thinking tools, such as observing, visualizing, and empathizing, so that memory, knowledge, imagination, and feelings are understood and appreciated in a holistic way. This ability to unite parts into wholes is especially useful to scientists, athletes, actors, musicians, physicians, and artists. The related skill of **empathizing** helps students to find within themselves a reflection of the outer world.

How to Use *The Whole-Brain Solution*

Higher-order thinking tools are interconnected, and have a place in every subject within the curriculum, and in life outside the school as well. The creative thinking tools in *The Whole-Brain Solution* do not really have a sequence; that is, you do not necessarily have to work with one tool before going on to another.

Each chapter includes

- **Lesson Plans** focusing on development of a creative thinking tool and a related skill
- **Two sections**, each with a **Warm-up** Activity (a quick introductory activity that begins each section) and a **Great Examples** Activity (the final activity in each section, which features the accomplishments of great creative individuals)
- A student's **Self-Assessment** of the featured tool and skill
- **Reproducibles**
  Strategy Spots   strategy summaries and tips for using them
  Worksheets   activities that can be collected and assessed
  Quotes and Notes   activities based on quotations
  Overhead Projections illustrations that can be displayed or distributed

Lesson Plans feature

- **Synopsis:** a brief overview of the focus of each lesson plan

- **Extension:** suggestion for going deeper into the lesson's topic
- **Challenge:** more difficult or time-consuming questions or activities
- **(Subject) Connection:** cross-curricular links to a range of subjects (Art, Career, Drama, Language Arts, Mathematics, Movement, Music, Science, Social Studies, and Technology). A full Index of Subject Connections can be found on page 143.
- **"See also":** other applicable lesson plans in *The Whole-Brain Solution* and useful resources for a particular activity

When and how can I use higher-order thinking tools?

There are many ways to use this book. You can mix and match any of the activities to suit your teaching style. You do not have to try to teach all of the tools all of the time. Simply be aware of these tools and alert for ways to incorporate them into daily lesson plans.

The activities in this book can be integrated easily into a wide variety of topics and subjects you are already teaching. Or you can devote separate class time to develop these tools with your students. You may find it helpful to have other teachers aware of your students' use of these tools. Your fellow teachers can reinforce connections in the subjects they teach. Perhaps a school-wide Thinking Tool of the Week (Month) could be instituted.

In your own classroom you may wish to

✓ Make a list of thinking tools. Post the list on a wall that is visible from all parts of the classroom. You may want to distribute copies of **Checklist: Thinking Tools** (page 11) to students. Or, you can post the tools as you introduce them to your class.

✓ Set aside a brief "Thinking Tool Time" each week and choose an activity at random.

✓ Choose a Thinking Tool Theme of the week or month, and reinforce that tool through activities from this book and connections made in other activities.

✓ Familiarize yourself with the tools in this book. When planning a lesson, choose the most appropriate tool and select an activity and/or reproducible to integrate into the lesson.

✓ Use the **Subject Connections** in the Index to find the activities specific to your subject area.

✓ Use any of the margin **quotations** to initiate class discussions to discover a deeper understanding of the topic being taught. You might like to add your own favorite quotations to the margins of this book and encourage students to start their own collection of quotations.

✓ Use the **Reproducibles** whenever and however they might be relevant or appropriate.

✓ Use just the **Warm-ups** and/or **Great Examples** from each chapter.

✓ Start at the beginning of the book and work through chapter by chapter.

✓ Find ways to reinforce the recurring themes in *The Whole-Brain Solution*
   - be open to all possibilities
   - everything relates to everything else
   - identify and go beyond assumptions

- change your perspective to view issues, topics, and subjects in different ways
- find a common link between two dissimilar things
- look beyond the first right answer
- the 'artist' and 'scientist' in each of us (subjective and objective experience) improve by being integrated

Are my students ready for these tools?

Children are ready to move from thinking about things to thinking about thinking by about age 10-12. By this time, they may already using higher-order thinking tools, though perhaps unconsciously. From this point onward students (and adults) can actively engage and develop their use of these tools to increase their creative thinking skills.

Am I ready to teach these tools?

Yes! This is not a field in which you need advance preparation — you can sharpen and refine your skills as you teach. Have fun. You may wish to distribute a copy of **Checklist: Thinking Tools** (on page 11) and/or **Checklist: 150 Ways to Use Information** (on page 12) to your students, either now or at any time during the year. These checklists will encourage students to be more aware of the strategies they use every day for integrating information.

Name: _____

Checklist: Thinking Tools

Use this checklist to help you identify the thinking tools that you use. Check off a thinking tool when you use it. Once you have checked all the tools, choose one skill each day and find a way to use it.

❏ **1. Observations**
Observations are facts that you learn directly through your senses. You can use what you see, hear, touch, taste, and smell to help you understand and remember information. Careful observation is an important skill for artists, scientists, naturalists, doctors, actors, and writers.

❏ **2. Generating Ideas**
Generating ideas means coming up with ideas about something. You can use your abilities to brainstorm, imagine, and recall to think of a wide variety of solutions and ideas. Skills in generating ideas are especially important in business, the fine arts, design, city planning, government, and problem solving.

❏ **3. Asking Questions**
Asking questions is an important part of learning because it increases your interest and helps you to connect information with your prior knowledge and experience. Skill in questioning is important in the fields of research, medicine, counseling, police work, marketing, and design.

❏ **4. Connecting**
Connecting is the ability to find links between things and to appreciate new combinations. Teachers, philosophers, artists, inventors, medical researchers, counselors, and architects call upon their connecting skills in everyday life.

❏ **5. Making Analogies**
An analogy is a comparison between two objects, ideas, or processes that have some qualities in common. For example, you can use something familiar to explain something unfamiliar (such as comparing a camera to an eye). Poets, visual artists, inventors, scientists, mathematicians, and humorists make regular use of analogies in their work.

❏ **6. Recognizing Patterns**
Recognizing patterns is a skill of seeing how parts fit together to make a whole. Pattern skills are important scientific and artistic tools and are used in medicine, engineering, dance, music, art, math, and languages.

❏ **7. Solving Problems**
Solving problems includes identifying a question and possible solutions and then selecting the best one. Problem-solving skills are called upon in every walk of life, especially in the legal professions, counseling, police work, city planning, engineering, architecture, medicine, and business.

❏ **8. Transforming**
Transforming is the process of changing information from one form into another. It is especially useful in teaching, engineering, designing, architecture, computing science, medicine, visual arts, and math.

❏ **9. Synthesizing**
Synthesizing is the process of putting together information together to create something new. The ability to unite parts into wholes is especially useful to actors, scientists, athletes, musicians, physicians, and artists.

❏ **10. Other thinking tools you know:**

_____

_____

_____

Name: _____

Checklist: 150 Ways to Use Information

How many ways can you use information? Probably more than you realize. Every day for the next few months, check off an information skill when you use it. At first it will be easy to check off skills, but eventually you will find some new skills that you can learn how to use. Once you have checked them all, choose one skill each day and find a way to use it.

- ❏ abstract
- ❏ acquire
- ❏ adapt
- ❏ analogize
- ❏ analyze
- ❏ animate
- ❏ apply
- ❏ appreciate
- ❏ approximate
- ❏ assemble
- ❏ assess
- ❏ average
- ❏ blend
- ❏ brainstorm
- ❏ browse
- ❏ catalog
- ❏ categorize
- ❏ celebrate
- ❏ choose
- ❏ chunk
- ❏ classify
- ❏ cluster
- ❏ collaborate
- ❏ collect
- ❏ combine
- ❏ compare
- ❏ comprehend
- ❏ communicate
- ❏ conceptualize
- ❏ conclude
- ❏ condense
- ❏ connect
- ❏ contrast
- ❏ clarify
- ❏ classify
- ❏ create

- ❏ decide
- ❏ describe
- ❏ design
- ❏ display
- ❏ distinguish
- ❏ distribute
- ❏ draft
- ❏ draw
- ❏ edit
- ❏ empathize
- ❏ enjoy
- ❏ estimate
- ❏ evaluate
- ❏ examine
- ❏ expand
- ❏ experience
- ❏ experiment
- ❏ explain
- ❏ explore
- ❏ focus
- ❏ gather
- ❏ generate
- ❏ graph
- ❏ group
- ❏ harmonize
- ❏ highlight
- ❏ hypothesize
- ❏ identify
- ❏ image
- ❏ imagine
- ❏ infer
- ❏ inform
- ❏ inquire
- ❏ inspect
- ❏ integrate
- ❏ interpret

- ❏ intuit
- ❏ investigate
- ❏ learn
- ❏ list
- ❏ locate
- ❏ look into
- ❏ make decisions
- ❏ map
- ❏ measure
- ❏ merge
- ❏ model
- ❏ observe
- ❏ order
- ❏ organize
- ❏ outline
- ❏ pair
- ❏ paraphrase
- ❏ picture
- ❏ plan
- ❏ play
- ❏ ponder
- ❏ predict
- ❏ question
- ❏ rationalize
- ❏ rearrange
- ❏ reason
- ❏ recognize
- ❏ record
- ❏ reduce
- ❏ refine
- ❏ relate
- ❏ remember
- ❏ represent
- ❏ research
- ❏ review
- ❏ revise

- ❏ role-play
- ❏ scan
- ❏ select
- ❏ sequence
- ❏ share
- ❏ simplify
- ❏ skim
- ❏ solve problems
- ❏ sort
- ❏ speculate
- ❏ storyboard
- ❏ structure
- ❏ substitute
- ❏ summarize
- ❏ symbolize
- ❏ synopsize
- ❏ synthesize
- ❏ take it apart
- ❏ teach
- ❏ test
- ❏ theorize
- ❏ transform
- ❏ understand
- ❏ use
- ❏ visualize
- ❏ other information skills you have used

CHAPTER 1   Observing

Observations are facts learned directly through the senses. Students can
improve their ability to observe from a variety of perspectives, and to visualize
and recall with increased clarity. Careful observation is an important skill for
artists, scientists, naturalists, doctors, actors, and writers. The related skill of
visualizing helps students form an image of what they are learning, recall
things visually, and imagine how things might look in the future.

Becoming More Aware

1.01 Warm-up

*Synopsis: Students practise seeing with a fresh perspective and explaining different
types of seeing.*

*The voyage of discovery is not in
seeing new landscapes but in
having new eyes.*
Marcel Proust

Ask students to choose an object on their desk and look at it closely. Prompt
them to gradually adjust their vision to focus on objects farther away. Then
have students scan back and forth over the entire scene. Ask students: *What
does it mean to see something? What do you know about the process of seeing in
terms of the functioning of the eyes and brain?* Students may mention that they
can look at things up close and far away, examine small details, or see the "big
picture" (insight). Ask students: *What is meant by the expression "Now I see!"?*

   Looking is the beginning of seeing, but to really see into the reality of a thing
the observer needs to consider many elements. The observer needs to be alert to

see what he or she has not seen before. Ask students: *What is in your sight right now? Look at it as if you are seeing it for the first time. Say to yourself, I don't yet know that object. I've seen it before, but I was different then, and now I might see a quality that I missed before.* Then discuss experiences.

As a group, have students create a list of synonyms for seeing, e.g., looking, beholding, observing, watching, viewing, perceiving. Challenge students to examine subtle differences among the meanings by creating a definition for each word and using each word in a sentence. Have students share their definitions and sentences to highlight the differences among the words.

1.02 Viewing the World

Synopsis: Students practise looking closely at objects using viewers.

Ask students: *How could you practise careful looking?* Discuss that a good way to look at an object carefully is to take the object out of context and examine it by itself. Have students use a magnifying glass or a camera (no film necessary) to view objects closely. Alternately, students can create a simple viewer such as an empty 35mm slide holder or a similarly-sized piece of cardboard with a hole cut out, or an empty toilet paper roll. Encourage students to look at whatever is within the frame: parts of their desk, photographs, floors, walls, trees, grass, and so on. They may find that ordinary things, such as cracks in the concrete, designs on tree bark, and patterns in brick walls, become fascinating. Ask: *How does using a viewer change what you notice about an object?* If possible, dim the lights or open/close the blinds (if outdoors, move into the shadows then into the sunlight). Ask: *How does a change in light change what you view?*

Students can draw what they see in their viewer. Post the drawings and have other students guess the objects.

Career Connection: Ask students: *Which occupations can you name that require a well-developed ability to observe?* (baseball players, detectives, photographers, pilots, surgeons) List the occupations and then ask students to brainstorm well-known people from each occupation. Have students choose one person then write a three-paragraph description detailing why they chose that person and describing an example that shows their skills of observation.

1.03 Contour Drawing

Synopsis: Students make contour drawings to practise recording what they see.

Ask students: *What do you know about contour drawing?* Contour drawing is a useful skill for drawing maps in Social Studies, recording what is viewed through the microscope in Science, and drawing geometric shapes in Math. And although it is a drawing technique, it is also a seeing technique. Contour drawing is a slow way of drawing. The artist looks almost exclusively at the object being drawn, not back and forth between the object and the paper. In fact, sometimes contour drawing is done with a divider placed so that the eye cannot see what the hand is drawing. Separating the processes of creating and analyzing helps students avoid being judgmental while they are being creative and spontaneous.

Supporting Learning: Check that the definitions show an understanding of different shades of meaning. ESL students can refer to "seeing" words in their first language.

Look beneath the surface: never let a thing's intrinsic quality or worth escape you.
Marcus Aurelius

Supporting Learning: Check that students only draw what is in the viewer, not the complete objects.

Familiar things happen, and mankind does not bother about them. It requires a very unusual mind to undertake the analysis of the obvious.
Alfred North Whitehead

14

Have students create a contour drawing. This is an exercise in seeing, and the shape of the finished drawing, even if very different from the object, will reflect qualities of the object. A good subject for students to start with is their hand or shoe. Have students choose a starting point on the object and on the paper and then slowly draw the outline on the paper as their eye moves around the object at the same speed. Caution students not to let the pencil get ahead of the eye or vice versa. Since they are not looking at the line they are drawing, they will have to make some decisions intuitively. (No erasers are allowed.) Advise students not to lift their pencil from the paper.

Encourage students to make contour drawings of the same object several different ways (clockwise, counter-clockwise, top to bottom). As students view their finished drawings, discuss what qualities in the sketches provide a sense of the object they drew. Ask: *What was difficult about this activity? What was surprising about the drawings? How can you use this skill in other ways?*

Supporting Learning: Students might need some encouragement to let go of the idea that they should make the drawing look a certain way.

1.04 Seeing Spaces

Synopsis: Students practise seeing spaces in and around objects by making drawings.

Place a chair on a desk or in the centre of the classroom where all students can see it. Ask: *How would you describe this chair?* Have students make a sketch of the chair. Then ask students to observe the space in and around the chair (between arms and legs, in between ornate patterns, perhaps in the back of the chair). Ask: *What shapes does the space make in and around this chair?* Have students sketch the spaces. Remind them that the goal is not to draw a realistic chair – it is to draw realistic spaces. Afterwards discuss: *How has this activity changed your way of viewing the chair?* Seeing spaces helps to break assumptions about the solidity or non-changing aspects of what is perceived.

Ask students to use other ways to draw the chair, such as contour drawing (see 1.03: Contour Drawing), upside down, one continuous line without lifting their pencils from their pages, and so on.

Extension: Discuss the importance of spaces in sounds (e.g., pauses in a conversation, pauses between songs on a CD, rests between musical notes).

See also: 6.03 Recognizing Nothingness

A vessel is useful only through its emptiness. It is the space opened in a wall that serves as a window. Thus, it is the nonexistent in things that makes them serviceable.
Lao-tse

Supporting Learning: Check that sketches show some variation among the different ways of drawing. The point is not to make "accurate" drawings, but to experience different ways of looking at space and form.

1.05 Using All Your Senses

Synopsis: Students practise observing objects closely and appreciating their qualities.

Pass around a natural object, such as a large pine cone, sea shell, or plant. Have each student describe one quality in a sentence as she or he handles it. (Caution students not to taste the object.) Each description should be different. Encourage students to look at the object from all angles, and consider its smell, texture, color, shape, and so on. Emphasize that the five physical senses provide a lot of information for the brain to process. Becoming more aware of the input from each of the senses means gaining more information about what is perceived. For example, an experienced cheese taster can determine all sorts of information about a piece of cheese from the taste and texture. A classical music enthusiast can notice the melody of the cello, even though the brass

What led me to my science and from my youth filled me with enthusiasm is the fact ... that our laws of thinking conform with the lawfulness in the passage of impressions which we receive from the outer world, thus making it possible for man to gain information about lawfulness by mere thinking.
Max Planck

instruments are playing louder. Collectors, connoisseurs, and experts find that their senses can make finer and finer distinctions in variation and quality.

Supporting Learning: Students may need more practice in noticing details. Discussing the lists will help students realize the number of details that can be observed.

Select another natural object, and ask students to handle it for several minutes, to examine its form, feel its texture, and consider its color and its smell. Then remove the object and have students recall as many details of the object as possible. Students can draw the object, list its qualities, etc. Bring out the object again so students can note what they missed in their descriptions and add to their lists/drawings in another color. Have students share their drawings or lists. Ask: *What things were easy/difficult to recall? Why do you think so?*

See also: 9.02 Linking Physical Senses

Extension: The information the senses send the brain is always relative. For instance, objects that are closer appear larger than objects that are farther away. A whisper sounds louder in a quiet classroom than in a noisy one. To become more aware of the information the senses are sending to the brain it may help to separate some of the information. Students could watch a few minutes of a video without the sound, then "watch" the video with the sound, but no picture. Discuss what they notice in each instance.

1.06 What Do You See?

Synopsis: Students practise visualizing, and note the connection between mental images and emotions.

When I get an idea I start at once building it in my imagination. I change the construction, make improvements, and operate the device in my mind. It is absolutely immaterial to me whether I run my turbine in my thought or test it in my shop. I even note if it is out of balance.
Nikola Tesla

Ask: *How can someone "see" the future?* Give students a moment to consider this question and then suggest that not only can we see the future, but we can also improve our ability to see it. An architect 'sees' the building before it is built, students can 'see' themselves at the beach long before summer holidays begin, and a basketball player 'sees' the shot before she shoots it. The ability to visualize, or to form an image, helps us to recall things visually and imagine how they might look in the future. Ask: *How might chemists use the ability to visualize?* (to see how molecules are linked together) *Interior decorators?* (to see how the room will look rearranged) *Chess players?* (to plan strategy) *When have you used the ability to visualize?* Have each student create a list of three examples to share with the class. Discuss students' examples together.

A mental image is a representation of physical objects or of abstract ideas (happiness, beauty). We see mental images all day long, and they help to create our inner world and our outlook on life. Many successful people have discovered that by directing their inner imagery they can improve their performance and achievements. Share this proverb with students: "What you see, you become." Ask: *What examples of this proverb have you noticed in your experiences? When has mental imagery affected your performance or achievements? How did the mental imagery affect your feelings?* (Students may have pictured themselves victoriously crossing the finish line of a race, or seeing an "A" grade at the top of a test and felt pride. They may have pictured themselves in a negative social situation and felt disheartened or depressed.) *How could you use mental imagery to improve your achievements?*

Supporting Learning: Students may be more comfortable answering these questions with a journal entry.

Invite students to practise refining their ability to visualize by having them imagine a computer monitor or television screen within their brain, with controls for adjusting focus, brightness, and size. They can choose an object, such as a slice of pizza, and try to see it clearly on their screen. (It may help to close their eyes. They can answer the following questions mentally as you read them, pausing after each instruction.)

Imagine you have a television screen in your brain and it is displaying a piece of pizza. Picture the bright red tomato sauce and the cheese melting down the side.

Mentally adjust the focus control to make the image blurry.

Now adjust the focus to make it clear again.

Slowly move the pizza further away.

Now slowly bring it forward for a close-up shot.

How does the pizza taste? How does it smell? Are you getting hungry thinking about it?

How does the crust feel when you pick it up with your (mental) hand?

How hot is it when you bite into it?

Now suppose someone hands you an ice cube. What is this sensation like?

Ask students to share their experiences. Some students may have noticed that images appeared slowly. Others may have found that they appeared all at once. Ask students: *What surprised you about this activity?* Forming clear and complete mental images can help students to be more aware of what they observe. Ask: *How can you put this skill to use?* Discuss and compare responses.

Extension: Students are probably familiar with playing Pin the Tail on the Donkey or Blind Man's Bluff. These games call upon the players to use an "inner" eye to determine where to move. There is a famous story about a Zen archer who stepped onto the archery field at midnight on a moonless night and shot an arrow to a target far away. He declared that the arrow had hit the centre of the target, and then he walked away. His amazed student groped through the darkness to find the target and discover that the arrow was, indeed, in the center. How did the archer hit the target? He had hit it many times in the daylight, so only needed to visualize it in his mind's eye.

Your students might like to do something similar, such as throwing a sponge ball into a wastebasket. Have students practise with their eyes open until they have the feel of just how far and how hard to throw. Then have them try again blindfolded. Encourage them to practise "seeing" where the basket is before tossing the ball. Ask: *How did you sense where and how to throw with your eyes closed? How else could you use this skill?*

See also: 8.04 Making Models, Math Connection; 9.01 Warm-up; 9.02 Linking Physical Senses; 9.04 Great Examples: If I Were an Electron

1.07 What Do You Recall?

Synopsis: Students practise short-term recall.

Ask students: *How would you rank your ability to recall information on a scale of 1 (can never recall anything) to 10 (can always recall everything)?* Here is an activity which can check short-term recall ability. Tell students: *It is said that the best conversations are those in which you respond to ideas, not words. Sometimes we miss the ideas because we haven't really heard the words. Do you really hear what is said in a conversation? Use this activity to sharpen your ability to understand what a person is really saying.* Have pairs of students select a book (such as a textbook) and sit facing one another. One student chooses a sentence at random from the book, reads it silently, and then repeats it aloud while looking at his or her partner. The partner then repeats the sentence. If the

Supporting Learning: If students have difficulty with this activity, ask: *What do you see when you think of pizza? Describe how it looks to you. What other details do you notice?*

Supporting Learning: The 'aim' of this activity is to increase students' sense of mind-body coordination, not to throw perfect tosses.

The greatest compliment that was ever paid me was when someone asked me what I thought and attended to my answer.
Henry David Thoreau

Supporting Learning: As you read the completed worksheets, look for descriptions that include all five senses.

partner is unsure or makes a mistake, the student repeats the sentence. Once the partner has succeeded in repeating the sentence correctly, the student can choose another sentence. Repeat this several times, and then change roles.

Encourage students to mentally repeat what they have heard in a conversation before responding. You may have found it helpful to have students repeat assignments after you announce them, just to make sure they have actually "heard" the words. Students can complete Worksheet 1A: **What Do You Recall?** to evaluate their ability to recall.

See also: 1.08 Tips for Memorizing and Recalling; Strategy Spot 1B: **Tips for Recalling**; 9.03 A Natural Act

1.08 Tips for Memorizing and Recalling

Synopsis: Students practise short-term recall and learn memorizing and studying tips.

I myself have proved it to be of no little use when in bed in the dark to run the imagination over the surface delineations of forms previously studied, or other remarkable things encompassed with subtle speculation. This is really a most praiseworthy activity and one that is useful for fixing things in the memory.
Leonardo da Vinci

Ask students: *What strategies have you used to help you remember something? What works best for you?* Discuss these points:

✓ One way to remember something is to relate what you are learning to something you already know. You can do this by finding a pattern (arranging words in a sentence, or using a mnemonic device to consciously classify or reconstruct what you're trying to remember) or by asking questions to help you focus on details to remember them better. Brainstorming and remembering key words can also help to recall information that you have stored in your mind. (See 4.04 Maps of the Mind.) These techniques help you to reduce the amount you need to remember and make it easier to recall facts and events.

✓ Another way to make remembering easier is to visualize what you are learning. Make a list of familiar objects and attach something difficult to remember to each object. For example, students could remember the following rhyming list: one is a bun, two is a shoe, three is a key, four is a door, five is a hive, six is sticks, seven is heaven, eight is a gate, nine is a line, and ten is a pen. Then supposing they want to remember what to buy at the grocery store, (laundry soap, oranges, toothpaste, and milk) they would attach each item to one of the memorized objects with some sort of visual image. (One is a bun, which reminds me that the filling of the bun is white, just like laundry soap powder; two is a shoe which makes me think of orange shoes which reminds me of oranges; three is a tree which reminds me of something hard to chew and chewing means teeth which reminds me of toothpaste; four is a door which I picture having a flood of milk pouring over me when I open it). Have students practise using this technique to remember information relevant to one of their school subjects.

Supporting Learning: Reinforce the use of the "one is a bun" technique over several lessons and encourage students to use the technique outside of school.

Distribute and discuss Strategy Spot 1B: **Tips for Recalling**. Ask: *Which of these techniques have you used? What were your experiences?*

Extension: Ask students: *How is studying related to memorizing and recalling?* You might wish to have students represent "study, memorize, and recall" graphically, perhaps by comparing and contrasting them in a three-circle Venn diagram. Check that students have noted that a good place to begin with studying is by recalling what they already know about a subject, and that studying involves understanding the material rather than just memorizing it. You may wish to distribute and discuss Strategy Spot 1C: **Study Skills**, which outlines several study aids. Encourage students to add their own study techniques to the page.

    See also: 1.07 What Do You Recall?; Worksheet 1A: **What Do You Recall?**; 9.03 A Natural Act

Supporting Learning: Create a poster of the main points from Strategy Spot 1B and 1C. Post it in the classroom and remind students to use the strategies; discuss their results.

If you take a flower in your hand and really look at it, it's your world for the moment.
Georgia O'Keefe

1.09 Great Examples: Great Observers

Synopsis: Students find and consider examples of observation skills at work.

Ask students to consider this question: *How do people describe what they see?* Literary and non-fiction works can be wonderful sources that show readers how the author "sees" things. Ask students to share examples from their own reading that they felt had excellent descriptions. Share your own favorites. Some first hand accounts of wildlife observers are a good place to start, e.g., *Cry of the Kalahari* by Mark and Delia Owens, *Pilgrim at Tinker's Creek*, by Annie Dillard, or the poetry of William Wordsworth. You might wish to have students work in pairs to complete Worksheet 1D: **How Do Others See It?** in which students relate how a natural object is described from three different points of view.

    See also: 9.04 If I Were an Electron

Supporting Learning: Before assigning Worksheet 1D, work through an example with students. Check students' work for both research and summarizing skills.

What's Your Perspective?

1.10 Warm-up

Synopsis: Students use a new perspective to observe familiar surroundings.

Invite students to imagine a fabulous restaurant that serves delectable dishes of all types. Ask: *Would you choose the same dish to eat for each meal every day of the week? Why, or why not? How is choosing the same food all the time like considering only one point of view about something?*

    The purpose of learning is to discover the truth about the matter. Finding the truth means being open to many possible interpretations and perspectives (ways of looking at things). This may mean a re-examination of the obvious, a willingness to change ideas, and a curiosity in understanding how other people view the same phenomenon. Have students try this change in perspective: *Imagine that you have just arrived in this classroom from another world and all you are seeing is new to you. The letters of words appear as a foreign alphabet; labels and signs are shapes without meanings.* Have students take a few minutes to walk around the classroom, silently looking at objects, letters, and numbers. Ask: *How does this way of looking at things change your perspective of everyday objects?*

    See also: 1.11 How Do You Look at It?; 2.01 Warm-up; 2.05 Have You Seen My Elephant?; 3.08 Discovering; Strategy Spot 3B: **Keep an Open Mind**; 7.08 Breaking Assumptions

    Extension: Students can have fun developing ambidexterity by writing their signature with their non-dominant hand, writing with one hand and drawing with the other simultaneously, or trying mirror writing. Ask: *What do you notice*

It has long been an axiom of mine that the little things are infinitely the more important.
Sir Arthur Conan Doyle

Supporting Learning: If students find this activity difficult, ask them to describe an occasion when they went to an unfamiliar place (on vacation, a new store or restaurant). Ask: *How much more did you notice compared to a place you had been many times before?*

when you do these activities? How could you improve your abilities? How might these skills be useful in daily life? Students could take a poll of classmates to discover whether there is a correlation between dominant hand and dominant foot (the foot they would use to kick a ball, etc.). They can graph the results. Ask students: *How could you test for dominant eye, ear, and arm?*

1.11 How Do You Look at It?

Synopsis: Students consider how changes in perspective affect understanding.

Where the telescope ends, the microscope begins. Which of the two has the grander view?
Victor Hugo

Have each student stand, sit, or lie in a different position or at a different angle to some natural object (such as a tree if you are outdoors, or a large object if you are indoors). Ask them to describe the object from their vantage point. Together, compare descriptions from different vantage points. Ask: *What aspects change from different perspectives? From looking up? From looking down? From far away? From close up?* Rotate positions and observe again. What conclusions can students make about perspective and observations?

Ask students to imagine a frog sitting in the bottom of a well. Ask: *What does the frog see when it looks up?* (the sky) To the frog, the small circle of sky seems to be the whole sky, but if the frog came to the surface of the well it would discover a much bigger sky. Ask students how this analogy applies to their own process of learning. (When you are young, you see only a small piece of sky [knowledge/world], but this expands as you learn more.) Invite students to give an example of how their own knowledge grew in a specific subject. For example, students could describe what they learned about math as they grew older: "First I learned how to recognize numbers, then I learned to count, add, subtract, divide, multiply, and solve mathematical problems." Encourage students to show their knowledge graphically. They could represent their growth of knowledge as expanding circles and label the knowledge that was part of each. Then they could draw a larger circle to encompass all the other circles, and label it to indicate what future knowledge they might gain. Ask: *How does growing in knowledge change the way you view the world?*

See also: 1.10 Warm-up; 2.01 Warm-up; 2.05 Have You Seen My Elephant?; 3.08 Discovering; Strategy Spot 3B; **Keep an Open Mind**; 7.08 Breaking Assumptions

Social Studies Connection: Ask students to give examples of how perspectives in society have changed over time (styles of clothes, the role of women, etc.). Discuss with students some of the differences in perspectives among cultures (manners, religion, environment, etc.). Students might consider the difference between a perspective of some Aboriginal peoples, that humans are at the bottom point of an inverted triangle, with all life above them, and a commonly held "Western" viewpoint that humans are at the top point of a triangle with all other life forms below them. Ask: *How might each point of view affect how a person thinks and acts?*

Supporting Learning: To assess students' ability to appreciate other points of view, ask them to summarize all the arguments presented in the debate.

Language Arts Connection: Debates are a good way to reflect on other points of view, especially if students are representing a viewpoint different than their own. Even members of an audience can find their viewpoints changing through exposure to other sides of an issue. Instead of the two-sided "pro" and "con" of formal debates, you may wish to have students form three or more teams to give them experience in thinking about an issue from three or more perspectives. For example, you may wish to present your students with the following scenario. Imagine that a vacant building lot next to an old, established neighborhood is going to be used for building a large retail mall. Students can represent the viewpoints of people who have strong opinions about the mall's location: neighbors, building developers, shopkeepers, wildlife experts, and local leaders. Have students debate whether the mall should be built within the neighborhood or elsewhere.

Math Connection: If appropriate for the level of your students, discuss the difference between algebraic and geometric thinking. Discuss the point that most people prefer one to the other, but some people can switch easily between the two. Invite students to research which type of thinking some famous scientists and mathematicians primarily use(d) in their research and work.

1.12 Everything Flows

Synopsis: Students interpret an expression about change in the world.

Write this famous saying by Heraclitus on the board:

> You can't step into the same river twice.

Ask students: *What do you think this quotation means? Do you agree with it? Why, or why not?* Discuss its meaning from the points of view of the river continuing to flow, the person continuing to change, and the river being changed because the person has stepped into it. Ask: *How does each interpretation of this saying connect with the importance of keeping an open mind when learning about something?* (Even if you have studied a subject before, you are different now and there might be something different about the subject that you could learn.) You might wish to distribute and discuss Strategy Spot 1E: **Open to Learning**, which discusses techniques students can use to keep an open mind when approaching a subject or topic.

Science Connection: Introduce the insight from quantum physics that simply by observing a given phenomenon, the observer affects the object being observed. Have students research this concept and report to the class, giving an example from science or their own lives.

1.13 The Artist and the Scientist

Synopsis: Students consider an artistic and scientific perspective of the world.

Ask students: *How does learning about science help you appreciate the beauty of the world?* For example, by studying the nitrogen cycle, students discover how nitrogen aids in the growth of trees, plants, and vegetation. Then discuss how the study of art helps them appreciate the beauty of the world. Ask: *Who can better appreciate a flower, a scientist or an artist? Why?* Ideally, students will suggest that the two must be combined and balanced for full appreciation and understanding of life. Ask: *When have you used a mostly scientific way of looking at something? When have you used a mostly artistic way?*

Have students use a Venn diagram or a poem with two voices (parts) to show the similarities and differences of an artistic and scientific viewpoint.

Thought is always interested more in one part of its object than in another and …chooses all the while it thinks.
William James

Supporting Learning: Have students evaluate their use of the strategies featured in Strategy Spot 1E and, based on their self-evaluation, have students create a plan for improving their use of the strategies. Plan a time for students to assess their performance at a later date to report on their progress.

As soon as man does not take his existence for granted, but beholds it as something unfathomably mysterious, thought begins.
Albert Schweitzer

Supporting Learning: Look for evidence that students value both an artistic and scientific viewpoint. You might wish to discuss these concepts in terms of "objective" and "subjective" means of gaining knowledge.

1.14 Reflecting

Synopsis: Students consider the value of thinking in depth about a topic.

Discuss with students: *Describe a time when you got the answer to something just by thinking about it. How was the process different than remembering an answer?* Reflecting is the ability to think in depth about a topic, and to explore, compare, and integrate learning. Ask students: *Why do you think this process is called reflecting? In what ways is it similar to the reflection of a mirror?*

Have students complete Quotes and Notes 1F: **Thinking About Thinking**, in which students explore a quotation about thinking. Post the finished drawings, grouping them according to the quotations they represent. Encourage students to appreciate all the viewpoints displayed in the drawings.

Extension: Students can reflect on their own abilities to appreciate by working with a theme for the day. The theme can be an idea, such as beauty or friendship; an object, such as paper or a flower; or a geometric shape or color. They can record observations throughout the day of where they find the theme represented and then reflect on the role the theme plays in their life. Alternately, students can choose their own theme, and later discuss why the theme was or was not an easy/useful choice. More advanced students could choose a theme such as the Golden Mean or appearance versus reality.

Social Studies Connection: Students could research and reflect on how certain themes or symbols have been used throughout history and literature. For example, how have circles been used in celebrations of peoples around the globe?

Supporting Learning: Look for students' understanding that reflecting is a self-referral process; it does not require anything from outside of the student to be added.

1.15 Great Examples: Seeing Into Things

Synopsis: Students write about something that has expanded how they see things.

We, as we read, must become Greeks, Romans, Turks, priest and king, martyr and executioner; must fasten these images to some reality in our secret experience, or we shall learn nothing rightly.
Ralph Waldo Emerson

Ask students: *What historical figure can you name that has been responsible for bringing a change in perspective?* (For example, early explorers establishing that the world was not flat and that ships wouldn't fall off its edge.) Great creators can sometimes bring about a change in perspective by helping people to "see" into things. A few famous historical examples include the following. Pablo Picasso's breakthrough painting, "Les Demoiselles d'Avignon," was the first painting in Western art to show its subject from all sides at once. Architect Filippo Brunelleschi and painter Albrecht Dürer challenged the existing views regarding perspective and proportion. Scientists, such as Nicolaus Copernicus, perceived order in the solar system and challenged the prevailing thinking of their time. In modern times astronauts have shared their view of Earth from space. Ask: *What events, ideas, or people have changed your view of life?* Ask students to write about a person, event, or idea that expanded the way they thought or looked at things. Students may wish to record their thoughts in the form of a poem or a journal entry. Invite students to share their writings.

Supporting Learning: As you read students' writing, look for an explanation or reason why and how their perspectives were changed.

Name: _____

What Do You Recall?

How well can you recall information, events, and memories? Answer the questions below with complete sentences. As you complete the questions, notice how clear or foggy the memories are, and whether they come quickly or slowly.

1. What were you doing an hour ago? 12 hours ago? 24 hours ago?

_____

_____

2. What did you wear last Sunday?

_____

_____

3. What did you do the day you turned nine?

_____

_____

4. What is one of your earliest memories?

_____

_____

5. What is one of your clearest memories?

_____

_____

6. What is something you told yourself you would never forget?

_____

_____

7. What do you wish you could remember better?

_____

_____

8. Describe an occasion when your memory helped you.

_____

_____

9. How do you think you could improve your memory?

_____

_____

Tips for Recalling

If you want to improve what you get OUT of your memory, pay attention to what you put INTO your memory!

1. **Decide what it is you need to remember.**
   You may not have to remember all the information in front of you. Just focus on the terms or events or objects that matter.

2. **Figure out what the whole concept is that you want to remember, rather than trying to isolate the parts.**
   Get a feeling for the whole, then decide what the general themes are and remember those. You may find that making a concept map and visualizing the map is easier than remembering a list of words.

3. **Use prompts and cues to help you learn the material.**
   Use what works for you. Match the words you are learning to the melody of your favorite song. Mentally "hang" facts in different places of the room (when I look at the door it reminds me of...). Visualize the information, and visualize yourself remembering it later.

4. **Imagine you are a character or a part of whatever you are reading.**
   Take a few moments to picture the events, the other characters, the setting, and the action. How would you feel? What would you see, taste, and smell?

5. **Check your memory by recalling information as a practise.**
   You can do this soon after you have learned something new, and then every so often until you need the information. Every once in a while ask yourself what you want and need to remember from the past.

6. **Use new techniques for remembering.**
   Ask other people how they remember. Record the techniques here, and then practise them to discover which ones work best for you.

   _____

   _____

   _____

   _____

   _____

   _____

   _____

Worksheet 1B

Study Skills

You can train your mind to be more focused, to learn better and faster, and to recall information easier. Here are some steps to get you started.

1. **Start with what you know.**

   Before you start studying take a few minutes to record what you know about the topic. Use a concept map, a KWL chart, or another way of organizing your thoughts. (See steps for using a KWL chart below.) Include what you learned the last time you studied this subject, as well as information you knew before. Notice where there are gaps or holes in information. Mark these with a highlighter or circle them in a different color. Be watching for this information as you study.

   • Use a KWL chart.
   Make three columns on your paper. K (Know) is for what you know about the subject. Record everything you know about the subject in this column.

   The second column, W (Wonder), is for what you wonder about the subject, and for your questions about it. A good way to come up with questions is to visualize your subject. For example, if you are learning about volcanoes, picture what you already know. Imagine you are witnessing an eruption while traveling inside a volcano. What do you see? What is happening, and why? Note the gaps in your knowledge or places you are uncertain of the answers. Record these thoughts and questions in the second column under W (Wonder).

   The third column, L (Learned), is for recording what you learned and the answers to your questions under the W column.

2. **Give yourself a specific objective of what you want to learn.**
   Break a large chunk of text (such as a chapter) into smaller pieces (such as sections). Start by an overview of a section:

   ✓ note the headings and any boldfaced or italic sections;
   ✓ read the captions and look at the photographs;
   ✓ look at the features in the margins; and
   ✓ think about any questions that are raised in the text.

   Then consider what it is you are about to learn by reading the section.

3. **As you read, ask yourself, "What does this mean? What did I just learn? What don't I understand?" after every section.**

   Reread the paragraphs or sentences that didn't seem to make sense and consider them now that you have finished the whole section. If something still isn't clear, mark the point with a sticky note to come back to later or to ask about. If you find that your mind is wandering as you read, go back to the place where you last remember getting the meaning of the words and begin reading again from that point.

Worksheet 1C

Name: _____

How Do Others See It?

How do other people see the same thing? Choose a natural object such as an animal, flower, or fruit. Find three examples in songs, poetry, or art that show how the object is described. Include the source where you found the description and then write a one sentence description of how the object is portrayed.

1. Source: _____

   Description: _____

   _____

   _____

2. Source: _____

   Description: _____

   _____

   _____

3. Source: _____

   Description: _____

   _____

   _____

Read your one sentence descriptions for each of the above. Then write a new sentence that summarizes all three descriptions.

_____

_____

_____

_____

Now, turn your one sentence description into a poem. You can add or delete words, but keep the meaning of the sentence in the poem. Use the back of this sheet if necessary.

_____

_____

_____

_____

Worksheet 1D

Strategy Spot

Open to Learning

Use these techniques to open your mind to learning.

1. **Beware of approaching a subject with the attitude "I already know about this."**
   Remember that things are constantly changing, and you are not the same as you were when you thought about this subject the last time. You have grown in your understanding since then. There may be something new for you to appreciate or understand as a result. Try approaching the subject with the thought, "I don't know about this yet."

2. **Be more interested in finding the truth of the matter than showing you are right or "just getting it done."**
   Be genuinely curious about the subject you are learning about. Think of each experience as an opportunity to find another piece of knowledge to add to the collection your mind is making. Always be ready to learn. You never know when the universe will present you with the information you need.

3. **Be alert for information that might change the way you see or do things.**
   Have an interest in the ideas of other people, especially when those ideas are different from yours. *Why do they think the way they do?* If you can sympathize with another point of view, it will add to your understanding of an issue.

4. **Get the best possible evidence you can before you make up your mind.**
   Don't jump to conclusions based on surface appearances. Remember there are many ways of looking at an issue. Until you've considered three or more perspectives, you have not yet gotten to know your subject. Learn to listen to your own feelings about an issue as well as those expressed by others. Your point of view is valid and may not need changing, but it can be strengthened and improved by understanding all sides.

Worksheet 1E

Name:_____

Thinking About Thinking

Choose one of the quotations below. On another page, draw an illustration or cartoon of what the quotation means to you. Include the quotation with the illustration.

I keep the subject constantly before me, and wait till the first dawnings open slowly, by little and little, into a full and clear light.

Sir Isaac Newton

All my life through, the new sights of nature made me rejoice like a child.

Marie Curie

You don't understand anything until you learn it more than one way.

Marvin Minsky

It is not enough to have a good mind; the main thing is to use it.

René Descartes

When all think alike, no one thinks very much.

Walter Lippmann

The universe is full of magical things, patiently waiting for our wits to grow sharper.

Eden Phillpotts

The moment one gives close attention to anything, even a blade of grass, it becomes a mysterious, awesome, indescribably magnificent world in itself.

Henry Miller

If a man will begin with certainties, he shall end in doubts, but if he will be content to begin with doubts, he shall end in certainty.

Francis Bacon

Worksheet 1F

Name: _____

Self-Assessment: Observing

Use the middle column to write your answers to each of the following questions. At a later date, re-assess your skill in observing by completing the right hand column.

	Date:	Date:
1. Which of your five senses would you most like to strengthen? Why?		
2. Finish this sentence: My thinking is clearest when		
3. What is your plan for improving your memory?		
4. How can you improve your ability to pay attention?		
5. Which study skills would you like to improve? How will you improve those skills?		
6. How does seeing other perspectives help you in your schoolwork? In your daily life?		

CHAPTER 2

Generating Ideas

Multiple Perspectives

2.01 Warm-up; 2.02 Brainstorming; 2.03 Techniques of the Stars; 2.04 More than One Right Answer; 2.05 Have You Seen My Elephant?; 2.06 What if…?; 2.07 I Am a Part of All I Have Met; 2.08 Great Examples: Great Collaborators

Multiple Possibilities

2.09 Warm-up; 2.10 Playing with Ideas; 2.11 The Shape of Things to Come; 2.12 Abstractions 2.13 Great Examples: One Thing Leads to Another

Reproducibles

2A Strategy Spot: **Would You Mind a Brainstorm?**; 2B Strategy Spot: **Techniques of the Stars**; Quotes and Notes 2C: **A Universal Perspective**; Worksheet 2D: **Good News/ Bad News**; Worksheet 2E: **Creative Creations**; Strategy Spot 2F: **Keep Track of Ideas**; Worksheet 2G: **The Shape of Things to Come**; Self-Assessment: **Generating Ideas**

Generating ideas is the process of devoting attention to a subject, enlivening prior knowledge, and inspiring new thoughts. Generating ideas calls for divergent thinking, which involves originality, a search for information, and novel answers. The strategies in this chapter can help students stimulate creativity by breaking up predictable thinking patterns and inspiring a wider range of possibilities. Skills in generating ideas are especially important in business, the fine arts, design, city planning, government, and problem solving. The related skill of **abstracting** helps students reduce complicated to simple principles.

Multiple Perspectives

2.01 Warm-up

Synopsis: Students use various perspectives to solve a problem.

Discovery consists of looking at the same thing as everyone else and thinking something different.
Albert Szent-Györgyi

Ask students: *What do you think a genius is? What qualities might a genius have? Do you think everyone has moments when they could be called a genius? Why or why not?* Sometimes, what might be termed genius simply comes from finding a new perspective. Have students consider the following analogy (and possibly illustrate it): Your eyes are able to see depth due to the difference in point of view between the two eyes. Likewise, two or more perspectives of a subject can help you see deeper into the subject. Ask: *When have you found this to be true in your own life?* Discuss with students that when people are introduced to a new subject or idea, they often approach it using their usual way of perceiving or thinking. To be more open-minded and creative, one has to get "beyond" the usual way of seeing and thinking. It takes a conscious effort to view a subject from different perspectives.

The following activity helps people consider different ways of thinking and is often used in creative "think tank" seminars. Ask students to form into teams and provide each team with a pile of scrap paper. Tell them that you want to see which team can get the most paper airplanes over a pre-determined finish line in 3 minutes. (Use a piece of masking tape to mark the finish line on the floor about 4 or 5 metres or yards away.) Don't give students any further instructions or clarifications. Then let them go to it. (If they are worried about identifying their airplanes, each group can make a mark on their papers). Observe the results. Many times students will begin by carefully folding their paper into the usual paper airplane shape, but some students may catch on to the fact that the shape was not defined. A scrunched-up ball of paper could also be considered a paper airplane. They might also figure out a way to send many pieces flying at once. If these possibilities don't occur to students, then after the first contest ask students: *Are there different ways of creating paper airplanes? What shape of airplane might be faster and easier to make?* Give each group a few minutes to discuss how they will proceed. Then, do this activity a second time.

Afterwards ask students to explain the value of "getting beyond" the usual way of seeing and thinking. Ask: *How can you put this skill to use in your schoolwork and daily life?*

See also: 1.10 Warm-up; 1.11 How Do You Look at It?; 2.05 Have You Seen My Elephant?; 3.08 Discovering; Strategy Spot 3B: **Keep an Open Mind**; 7.08 Breaking Assumptions

Supporting Learning: Notice the ability of group members to support one another's ideas and to encourage creativity.

Not only strike while the iron is hot, but make it hot by striking.
Oliver Cromwell

2.02 Brainstorming

Synopsis: Students review and practise brainstorming.

Ask students: *What is a "brain storm"? What might a brain storm look like?* Discuss responses. Students could illustrate their answers. Ask students: *What experience have you had with brainstorming?* Together create a chart listing guidelines for brainstorming. Alternatively, you may wish to distribute, read aloud, and discuss Strategy Spot 2A: **Would You Mind a Brainstorm?**, which leads students through the steps of a brainstorming session.

Emphasize to students the importance of deferring judgment while generating ideas. The trick is to first produce many ideas and then, later, evaluate them. Ask students why they might brainstorm rather than just using the first or second idea that they think of. Compare the process to that of a farmer who harvests corn. Ask: *Does the farmer take just one cob of corn to the barn, or does he wait until he has a truckful of corn to return to the barn? Why? How does this analogy compare with generating ideas?*

In groups, have students use brainstorming to consider the following topic (or choose a topic relevant to a subject currently being studied): *How would you redesign the school?* Set a time limit of 5 minutes for the brainstorming session. Alternately, you might wish to split the class into two groups. One group can divide into smaller groups and proceed as outlined above. The members of the other group can each brainstorm on their own and after five minutes pool their results. Discuss which method students prefer (individual brainstorming and pooling, or group brainstorming) and which method seemed most effective.

Extension: Write a question or topic on a large sheet of paper and post it in the classroom. Encourage students to write their ideas under the topic from time to time during the day. They can read the ideas already provided to spur on their own thoughts. Post the topic for several days, so students will have more time to think of ideas.

2.03 Techniques of the Stars

Synopsis: Students consider others' techniques for generating ideas.

Ask students: *How do you come up with new ideas?* Students may say they break through their preconceptions about a topic, pay attention to unusual ideas rather than discarding them, and use ideas as stepping-stones to other ideas. Ask: *How are your experiences similar to the following experiences?*

> When I am, as it were, completely myself, entirely alone, and of good cheer — say, traveling in a carriage, or walking after a good meal, or during the night when I cannot sleep: it is on such occasions that my ideas flow best and most abundantly.— *Wolfgang Amadeus Mozart*

> You will ask me where I get my ideas. That I cannot tell you with certainty; they come unsummoned, directly or indirectly… in the silence of the nights, early in the morning.—*Ludwig van Beethoven*

Distribute and discuss Strategy Spot 2B: **Techniques of the Stars**, in which students consider three techniques for generating ideas that have been used by famous thinkers. Discuss student responses together.

See also: 3.09 What's the Chance?

Career Connection: Have students brainstorm how the ability to generate ideas might be useful in a career. Students can list four or five occupations that appeal to them and all the ways that generating ideas could be useful to each one. Ask students to share their responses in small groups and then add to their lists based on the feedback they receive.

2.04 More than One Right Answer

Synopsis: Students practise finding value in other viewpoints.

Ask students: *What is one opinion that you have that you think you will never change? Explain your reasons. What other opinions could there be for this same topic?* Have students discuss the quote in the margin by Emile Chartier. Ask: *What do you think it means? What might happen if you consider a new subject from only one perspective?* Have students work with a partner to discuss a community or school issue. One student can state a fact, and the other can say, "On the other hand…" and show there is truth in the opposite viewpoint.

If they have not already done so, have students complete and discuss activities 1 and 3 from Strategy Spot 2B: **Techniques of the Stars.**

Supporting Learning: Observe for group members' ability to create a "safe" environment for others' ideas and a willingness to accept and encourage contributions.

If I have done the public any service, it is due to patient thought.
Sir Isaac Newton

Supporting Learning: You may wish to assign each of the activities from Strategy Spot 2B over the coming days or weeks.

Nothing is more dangerous than an idea when it is the only one you have.
Emile Chartier

Supporting Learning: Some students will be more comfortable responding to the opening questions with a journal entry.

Science Connection: Albert Einstein suggested that the distinction between matter and energy might depend upon a point of view. What was a wave from one point of view was a particle in another. Ask students: *How can a body be at rest and in motion at the same time?* (It depends on your point of view.) Students could discuss this concept with a partner and devise a way of illustrating it (such as a person at rest in an elevator which is in motion, or a person at rest in a train which is in motion). They should include two perspectives in their illustration.

Art/Science Connection: Have students view Salvador Dali's work "Nature Morte Vivante" in which Dali integrated Albert Einstein's theory of relativity to show different objects simultaneously in motion and rest.

Social Studies Connection: Students could find examples of governments or leaders that show a willingness and ability to incorporate many perspectives into their decision-making. Ask: *How has considering various perspectives affected their policies, decisions, and the populations they represent?*

2.05 Have You Seen My Elephant?

Synopsis: Students illustrate or perform a fable about perspective.

Discuss with students: *Imagine that three blindfolded people are led to an elephant and asked to touch it and then decide what the object is they are touching. What might a person say who was feeling the elephant's side? What might the person say who was feeling the elephant's leg? The trunk? The tail?* The blindfolded people may say the elephant is like a wall, a tree trunk, or a snake. Ask: *Which view is correct? Why? How could more than one answer possibly be right? How does this story illustrate the importance of seeing different sides of an issue? What experiences of yours does this story remind you of?*

Have students create an illustration titled "More than One Right Answer" using the elephant story or their own example. Alternately, students can retell the story using examples from their own life, or they may wish to script and perform a version of the story.

See also: 1.10 Warm-up; 1.11 How Do You Look at It?; 2.01 Warm-up; 3.08 Discovering; Strategy Spot 3B: **Keep an Open Mind**; 7.08 Breaking Assumptions

Extension: Ask students: *How would you describe the universe?* Have students work alone or with a partner to complete the stem "The universe is…" Students should strive to capture how they see it, and not refer to a dictionary or other resource. They can share and compare their various perspectives and then complete Quotes and Notes 2C: **A Universal Perspective**, in which students read, reflect on, and illustrate quotations about the universe.

Art Connection: Ask: *Why might an artist create many views of the same object?* Have students find examples of artists who have worked with many views of one subject, for example, Paul Cézanne's multiple versions of apples on a tablecloth. Have students create a plan on how they will research this topic. Alternately, students can find examples of how ordinary things become art simply by changing one's perspective, such as when Pablo Picasso hung a bicycle seat and handle bars on a wall and they became a "bull's head." Have students share the examples they find with the class.

Gaining a wider perspective is like opening a window into a stuffy room — the whole atmosphere changes and the fresh breeze carries alternatives to our habitual ways of reacting.
Tarthang Tulku

Supporting Learning: ESL students may be aware of a similar story from their background that they could share with the class.

33

2.06 What if…?

Synopsis: Students consider "What if…?" scenarios.

A good way to generate ideas is to ask "What if…?" questions. Ask students: *What if time ran backwards? How would things change?* For example, forest fires would create huge forests — they would convert scorched, blackened soil into colorful flames, which as they diminished would be replaced by trees and other plants. Students could work alone or with a partner to generate another scenario of what might happen if time ran backwards (such as cars cleaning the air by sucking in exhaust, converting it to fuel, taking it to emptying stations so it could be returned to the earth). Students could create flow charts to illustrate their scenarios to the class. Ask: *How could you use "what if" questions in your own life?*

You may wish to have students complete Worksheet 2D: **Good News/ Bad News,** in which students consider different advantages and disadvantages to hypothetical situations.

2.07 I Am a Part of All I Have Met

Synopsis: Students create a self-portrait showing the major influences in their lives.

Read the margin quotation by Goethe to students. Discuss: *How does this quote apply to your life? What are some of the main influences that have contributed to your life?* (friends, family members, heroes, personal mentors) Students could create a self-portrait in any medium showing the influences that have contributed to who they are and write an accompanying caption explaining the portrait.

Extension: Ask students to consider whether they agree or disagree with the following quotation:

> Every man's work, whether it be literature or music or pictures or architecture or anything else, is always a portrait of himself.—*Samuel Butler*

Students can support their opinions with personal experiences and examples.
See also: 9.03 A Natural Act

Language Arts Connection: The title of this lesson, "I Am a Part of All I Have Met," is a line from a poem by Lord Alfred Tennyson. If appropriate to your students' level, have them research what poem this line is from ("Ulysses") and then have them read the poem. Ask students to create their own poems with this line as a title.

Science Connection: Students may be aware that the molecules in the air they breathe and the water they drink are the same molecules that existed in the time of the dinosaurs. Have students create an illustration showing how the molecules have traveled "through time" and have been "recycled."

Social Studies Connection: Read the following Sanskrit proverb to students: "The world is my family." Have students consider how this proverb applies to them. Ask: *In what ways can people of the world be considered members of your family?* Discuss as a group and then have students create a poster to illustrate the proverb.

Science advances, not by the accumulation of new facts…but by the continuous development of new concepts.
James Bryant Conant

Supporting Learning: If students find it difficult to complete Worksheet 2D, suggest that they start by listing the opposite of what is asked (for example, the good things about being popular). Then they can consider the reverse of each of the points they listed.

I have collected and used everything that I have seen, heard, and observed… Every one of my writings has come to me through a thousand different things.
Johann Wolfgang von Goethe

Supporting Learning: Look for a variety of influences shown in each self-portrait.

2.08 Great Examples: Great Collaborators

Synopsis: Students collaborate to read poetry.

"*Two heads are better than one.*" Ask students: *When have you seen the truth of this statement in action? What is the best work you have done with a partner or a team?* Have students brainstorm and/or research some famous collaborations of two or more people (Picasso and Braque, Lennon and McCartney, The Group of Seven, Watson and Crick, Marie and Pierre Curie, Steven Spielberg and George Lucas, Helen Keller and Annie Sullivan).

Supporting Learning: As students work on their poems, look for contributions from each partner.

Organize students into pairs to read and then perform a poem for two voices (such as one from *Joyful Noise: Poems for Two Voices*, by Paul Fleischman). Or, students can work with a partner to write and perform their own poem for two voices.

Multiple Possibilities

2.09 Warm-up

Synopsis: Students use Leonardo da Vinci's technique for generating ideas.

Ask students: *When have you noticed interesting shapes in clouds, mountains, trees, and so on? What did you see?* Discuss that when Leonardo da Vinci was searching for ideas, he would examine the shapes in clouds or stains on walls, in ashes of a fire, or patterns in mud. Sometimes he would throw a paint-soaked sponge against a wall and observe the resulting stains. He connected the shapes he saw to whatever subject he was thinking about.

Ask students to close their eyes and relax, then using a blank sheet of paper, begin writing random lines and scribbles on the page. Then have students open their eyes and search the scribbles for any images, symbols, structures, or patterns that occur to them and write down the first word that comes to mind for each. Encourage students to rotate the paper and look at the scribbles from different angles and continue to write down the words that come to mind. Students can then combine all their words to write a sentence or paragraph. Discuss results and what students found interesting, surprising, or helpful about the activity. Ask: *How might you use this technique in daily life?*

Supporting Learning: As students work, observe for a willingness to search for and interpret shapes. If students have difficulty finding images, ask: *What does the whole page of scribbles remind you of?*

See also: 5.02 A Close-up Look at Analogies; Worksheet 5A: **This Reminds Me**

Art Connection: Students can make monoprints (watercolor paint is applied to glass, then a paper is pressed onto the paint and the resulting arrangement of colors are analyzed). Ask: *What does the shape remind you of? What else does the shape remind you of?* Students could add some lines and more color to make an abstract representation of their subject, and post the picture and a few written lines explaining it.

2.10 Playing with Ideas

Synopsis: Students combine words and pictures to generate ideas.

So deep is the creative spirit that you will never discover its limits even if you search every trail.
Heraclitus

✓ Have students choose 10 words randomly from a dictionary or textbook or list 10 random words and exchange with a partner. Then have students write a poem, sentence, or description that uses all 10 words.

✓ Ask students to select three or four pictures from magazines that include a variety of people and situations. They can create a story that links the pictures, incorporating information from each of the senses that might be suggested by the pictures. Students could exchange their pictures with a partner and write about their partner's pictures, and then compare their stories.

✓ Reading "how-to" books and biographies can be a good source of ideas. Encourage students to borrow information from one field to help understand topics in other fields. For example, a student might apply knowledge of how to read a thermometer to help understand the study of integers in math.

Supporting Learning: Encourage students to make a plan for how they will keep track of their ideas (see Strategy Spot 2F). Check back in a few days to see how they are following their plans.

✓ Have students use Worksheet 2E: **Creative Creations,** in which students assign attributes (folding, glowing, hanging) to familiar objects (bicycles, suitcase, tent) to create possible inventions (such as a bendable, patterned calculator).

You may wish to distribute and discuss Strategy Spot 2F: **Keep Track of Ideas,** which lists techniques for recording ideas.

See also: 4.07 Combinatory Play

2.11 The Shape of Things to Come

Synopsis: Students use shapes and letters to generate forms.

Inventing is a combination of brains and material. The more brains you use, the less material you need.
Charles F. Kettering

Invite students to consider the shapes they like to doodle or draw. Ask students: *Which shapes have you always liked and used in your creations? What does each shape suggest to you?*

Ask: *What could you draw if you only used two squares and a triangle (of any size)?* Have students make some sketches, then share their results. Many students may have made a "house" shape. Encourage students to experiment with varying the size of one or more of the three components and to make other forms with them.

Supporting Learning: Students may benefit from having examples of the components displayed in the classroom, and from being paired with a partner who finds it easy to visualize three-dimensional designs.

Draw the following shapes on the board: in one section draw a circle, a triangle, and a square. In another section print the capital letters D, V, J, C, L, P and the number 8 (draw 8 as one circle above another). Tell students they have 15 minutes to make as many different creations as they can. Each creation must use at least one item, but no more than three, from each category. (You might wish to make one or two creations as a class before students work on them independently.) When students are finished, discuss the results and what they found easy and difficult about the activity. Ask students: *What skills did you use to complete this activity? How are these skills useful in other areas of your life?* Students could work with a partner to use Worksheet 2G: **The Shape of Things to Come,** in which they use several shapes to build a creation of their own choosing.

See also: 7.09 Sources for Inventions

2.12 Abstractions

Synopsis: Students practise recognizing and creating abstractions.

Teaching Note: Much of teaching involves taking abstract principles for specific disciplines and developing corresponding concrete learning activities. This is important because students do not learn through abstractions — they learn experientially. The following activities are not about teaching students to grasp abstract concepts; they are about how to take a concept or object, and through the process of abstracting, simplify it and appreciate it in different forms.

Ask students: *What are the rules of this classroom (school)?* Discuss the fact that rules are one example of abstracting, which means reducing complicated things to simple principles. Discuss some examples of abstracting, such as a half hour television show is abstracted in a one sentence summary in a TV guide, a movie title can be abstracted into gestures in a game of charades. Ask: *What other examples can you suggest?* (summary, précis, proverb, headline, personalized license plate)

Have students work in small groups to list abstractions connected with school activities. They can start by exploring the classroom (e.g., a Table of Contents is an abstraction of a book's contents, a list of Classroom Rules is an abstraction of the expected behavior). In each case they should indicate the abstraction, and what it is an abstraction of. Students can share and compare lists when they are finished. Ask: *How do you use your abstracting skills in daily life? How can you make more use of your abstracting skills? Why are these important skills?*

Challenge: A scientific experiment or theory is an abstraction, as is a painting or poem. Ask students: *What does a scientist have in common with an artist or a poet?* (One possible answer is that they each search for simple truths in the midst of complexity.) Ask: *How might scientists benefit from a method of abstracting developed by artists? How might artists benefit from a scientific discovery?* Then have students research how each field has benefited from abstractions in the other. Some research topics are perspective, chaos theory, and fractals. For example, the mathematical discovery of fractals has led to the creation of beautiful computer art, which has in turn suggested new avenues for mathematicians to exploration.

See also: 4.03 A Class Act; 4.05 Great Examples: One Field Helps Another; 4.06 Warm-up; 6.08 Playful Patterns

Art Connection: Have students choose a painting or color photograph to abstract. First, they can select the elements they consider the most important from their chosen photograph or painting. They can paint those elements, omitting details that are not essential. Then, students can choose another level of abstractness (such as making the painting monochromatic, or just painting the shapes of color) to create another painting. They can display their work next to the original painting, and discuss how their abstractions are similar to and different from the original.

Language Arts Connection: Any kind of summarizing is a form of abstraction, and there are many opportunities to summarize within Language Arts. Students may not have had much practice in abstracting an already abstract expression – a poem. Have students abstract a poem into a simpler poem, and then abstract the simpler poem again. They could continue until

---

The higher processes of art are all processes of simplification … That, indeed, is very nearly the whole of the higher artistic process; finding what conventions of form and what detail one can do without and yet preserve the spirit of the whole.
Willa Cather

Supporting Learning: As an ongoing activity, encourage students to consider the single most important message, principle, or key idea from any stories, lessons, or readings currently being studied. Watch for improvements in the ease and accuracy of abstracting.

I have observed that involvement with abstraction increases one's sensitivity to reality.
Oskar Schlemmer

they have just a noun, verb, and adverb or adjective. You might wish to first abstract a poem as a class and then have students abstract another poem on their own. Have students share their poems.

Social Studies Connection: Have a collection of various types of maps for students to compare and evaluate (e.g., road maps, atlases, globes, floor plans, maps from local attractions like museums, malls, or theme parks). Discuss how a map is an abstraction of what is represents. Discuss the meaning of the expression, "The map is not the territory." A map of a country is not a country, it is an abstraction that represents the country. Discuss: *What elements does each map contain? What makes a good map?* You may want to have students create a map of the school (or the classroom or their homes). Be sure students label the various parts of the map, such as office, library, entrances, playground, washrooms, and gym.

Science Connection: Ask: *Do you think a scientist prefers highly complex thoughts and ideas or simple, straightforward thoughts and ideas? Why?* Students may not realize that much of science is centered on simplifying and unifying theories about phenomenon. Scientists sometime speak of "elegant" theories, which although describing complexity, can be broken down into simple, easy-to-understand rules. Together list theories that students know (Dalton's atomic theory, theory of plate tectonics, cell theory, theory of evolution, theory of relativity). Ask: *Which theories do you think should be awarded the status of "elegant" (simple, easy to understand)?* Students can research to find other "elegant" theories.

> *Mathematics is the tool specially suited for dealing with abstract concepts of any kind. There is no limit to its power in this field.*
> Paul Dirac

Math Extension: Mathematics is filled with many examples of abstractions. Write the number 7 on the board and ask students: *What does this number represent? What is abstract about any number?* (It can be applied to anything, anywhere, at any time, without reference to objects.) *What is zero an abstraction of?* (That which does not exist but that holds the place of what could exist.) Have students find other abstractions in mathematics (such as formulas) and illustrate both the abstractions and what they are abstractions of.

See also: 7.07 Thinking it Through; Worksheet 7E: **Colorful Countries** and *The Most Beautiful Mathematical Formulas: 49 of the Most Interesting and Useful Mathematical Formulas*, by Lionel Salem et al.

Technology Connection: Animation is an abstraction of movement. Students may have some familiarity with "motion capture" technology and its use in movies and video games. Small sensors are placed on key points on a person's body and send spatial information into computers for use in creating animated figures. Have students discuss where they think sensors need to be placed and why. Then they can research this technology and share their information with the class. Students might enjoy abstracting motion by creating flip books in which a cartoon figure is shown gradually moving as the pages are flipped.

2.13 Great Examples: One Thing Leads to Another

Synopsis: Students contribute examples of how one thing leads to another.

There are a thousand thoughts lying within a man that he does not know 'til he takes up a pen to write.
William Makepeace Thackeray

Share the margin quotation by Thackeray with the students. Ask students: *When have you had an experience like Thackeray's?* Ask students to explain the following quotation from writer E.L. Doctorow:

Writing is like driving a car at night. You can only see as far as the headlights, but you make the whole trip that way.

Discuss: *What experiences does this quotation remind you of? What experiences have you had of the expression 'One thing leads to another'?*

Sometimes the best results come about because one idea or thought leads to another. For example, physicist Karl Jansky was studying ways to reduce telephone static so he built an antenna to help him in his work. Using the antennae he discovered radio waves from the Milky Way galaxy and launched the beginning of radio astronomy. Chemist William Perkin was researching how to create synthetic quinine to combat malaria. In doing so he discovered the first synthetic color, mauve, and launched a huge industry in synthetic dyes and colors. Vincent Van Gogh would start with a concept for a painting and create it in one session. Then he would create a whole series of paintings of the subject, each one leading him to some new aspect and showing him how to get closer to his original vision of the subject. Ask students to think of other examples (including from their own lives) of when one thing led to another. They can make an events chain to show the stages and connections of their examples.

See also: 4.05 Great Examples: One Field Helps Another

Supporting Learning: Check for understanding that achieving a goal does not always follow a "straight" path.

Would You Mind a Brainstorm?

Before Brainstorming

1. **Choose your topic.**
   If you are working with a group, read the topic aloud, so everyone knows exactly what to work with. A more specific topic works better than a general one. For example, "How can we improve the school's recycling program?" will produce better responses than "Recycling." Set a time limit.

2. **Appoint someone to record ideas.**
   The recorder simply records the ideas as they are given. (This would be yourself if you are working alone.) At this stage, there is no need to evaluate ideas or "correct" them — just record them as they come. Whatever is said (or thought, if you are on your own) goes on the list, no matter how unusual or impractical it might seem.

During Brainstorming

3. **Keep the ideas flowing.**
   Even if you get an idea you know is "good," do not stop to think about it. Use the whole time you have set aside only for generating ideas, not for developing them.

4. **Use ideas already mentioned to inspire new ideas.**
   You can change ideas, extend them, state the opposite, and so on.

5. **Encourage any and every idea.**
   Even the most "off the wall" idea might inspire a wonderful idea.

After Brainstorming

6. **Now is your chance to think about and develop your list.**
   There may be some ideas you can immediately discard, but before you do, consider whether some element of the idea might work. Encourage thinking like, "That reminds me of..." Sometimes the idea that everyone dislikes or thinks has no merit has some seed of an idea within it that can be used.

7. **If you're not sure of what ideas to keep and which to discard, have the group vote for their two or three favorite ideas.**
   Discard the ideas that did not get any votes. Work with the remaining ideas, having another vote if necessary.

8. **Remember, you do not have to choose a "usual" idea.**
   Just because an idea worked in the past doesn't mean it is the best idea for the future.

Worksheet 2A

Name: _____

Techniques of the Stars

Great creative thinkers do not just have random creative ideas — they use tricks and techniques to make them happen. Use one, two, or three of these techniques and you, too, can become an Ideas Star!

1. Leonardo da Vinci felt that he needed to view a subject from at least three different perspectives before he had a basis for understanding it. He would then combine the perspectives and reconsider his subject. Make a habit of doing this in your daily decision making. Consider three different perspectives of the situation, and then look for a way to combine the different perspectives. Try this technique on your own, then write about your experience here:

   _____

   _____

   _____

   _____

2. Drawing teacher Betty Edwards suggests that drawing something upside down is an excellent way of breaking assumptions about a subject, because the side of the brain that likes to label and limit experience has to take a back seat to the creative side. Practise this technique by turning a simple picture upside down and drawing it. As you draw do not name what the line is, just consider it a line joining to another line. Do not turn your drawing right side up until you are finished. You will find this activity will help open your mind to new ways of thinking about things. Try the technique of drawing upside down, then write your comments about it here:

   _____

   _____

   _____

   _____

3. Walt Disney would break thinking about ideas into three parts: dreamer, realist, and critic. First, he would generate ideas and dreams without worrying about whether they could work. The next day he would look for ways to make a dream idea something that would work and be practical. The third day he would view the idea from a critic's point of view to see what might need refinement. Try this technique with an idea of your own, then write your comments about it here:

   _____

   _____

   _____

   _____

Name: _____

A Universal Perspective

What do you think when you think about the universe? Complete this sentence:

The universe is _____
_____
_____
_____

Choose one of the following quotations (or your own quotation about the universe) and illustrate it.

In some sense man is a microcosm* of the universe; therefore what man is, is a clue to the universe.

David Bohm

*miniature version

The universe is wider than our view of it.

Henry David Thoreau

The universe is change; our life is what our thoughts make it.

Marcus Aurelius

The universe is made of stories, not atoms.

Muriel Rukeyser

Worksheet 2C

Name: _____

Good News/Bad News

Winning the lottery is good, right? Losing a job is bad, right? Are you sure? Take a closer look at your assumptions by responding to the following scenarios.

1. You have just been voted the most popular person in the school. List three difficulties it might cause.

   _____

   _____

   _____

2. You have just been given an earlier bedtime. List three good things that might happen as a result.

   _____

   _____

   _____

3. You have been given a $500.00 a month allowance. List four difficulties it might cause.

   _____

   _____

   _____

4. You have just discovered you have to leave all your friends and enroll at a new school. List five good things that might happen as a result.

   _____

   _____

   _____

5. Write your own example and exchange with a partner:

   _____

   _____

   _____

   _____

   _____

Worksheet 2D

Name: _____

Creative Creations

Cut this page into three columns and place the columns side by side. Move any of the columns up or down and visualize the creation that results (e.g., spinning electric shoe? glowing inflatable suitcase?). Then add your own ideas to the bottom of each list and move the columns again. Record your three favorite creations and make a sketch of each on another page.

bendable	musical	bicycle
spinning	patterned	pencil
stretched	electric	suitcase
compressed	magnetic	calculator
folding	inflatable	scissors
glowing	collectable	sunglasses
floating	edible	skateboard
hanging	recyclable	shoe
twistable	rechargeable	hammer
soft	unbreakable	tent

Worksheet 2E

Strategy Spot   Name:_____

Keep Track of Ideas

Why is it important to write down your ideas? Think about the following quotation.

> Look sharply after your thoughts. They come unlooked for, like a new bird seen
> on your trees, and, if you turn to your usual task, disappear.
> - *Ralph Waldo Emerson*

Have you had ideas that have disappeared? Try one or more of these techniques for keeping track of ideas.

1. Container

Keep a container of ideas. Collect whatever interests you — ads, quotes, designs, pictures, ideas, questions, cartoons, and put them in your container. Shake up the container and pull out several at a time whenever you need inspiration. Consider how the items you pulled out could apply to your topic.

2. Notebooks

Thomas Edison, an inventor, worked on over 50 inventions at a time. How did he keep track of his ideas? He wrote them down in a notebook as soon as he thought of them, whether in the middle of a conversation, at a meal, or out walking with friends. He would review his notebooks if he was stuck on an idea and wanted a new approach, or if he wanted to rethink an invention he had abandoned earlier. Edison also recorded ideas and inventions by other people that he could use or improve on. Over 3000 of his notebooks still exist and you can view parts of them by researching at the library or on the Internet. While you're researching, take a look at Leonardo da Vinci's notebooks — they include lots of sketches for his ideas and some backwards (or mirror) writing.

Use a notebook to keep track of your ideas. When you review your notebook you will be surprised by ideas you had forgotten or answers to questions you did not know you knew. The key is to jot down your inspirations, insights, and ideas as they happen — do not count on remembering them later. Keep a notebook close at hand, because ideas can happen anywhere, any time.

3. Envelopes

Poet Walt Whitman recorded ideas on slips of paper that he filed in envelopes according to the subject. When he wanted idea starters, he would reach into the envelopes at random, or would go to the envelope about his topic, then weave the ideas together.

4. How else could you keep track of your ideas? List your techniques here.

_____

_____

_____

_____

Worksheet 2F

Name: _____

The Shape of Things to Come

Look at the shapes below. Imagine how these shapes would look in three dimensions. What could you build with them? What could you invent? Draw your creations on the back of this page. You can change the size of any of the shapes and use as many of each as you wish.

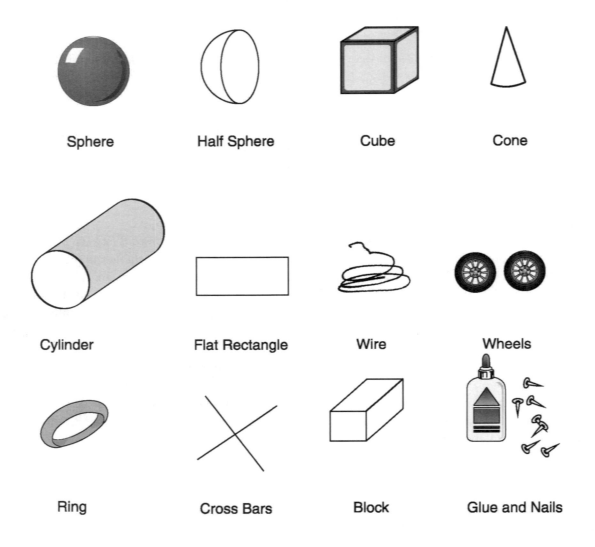

Sphere	Half Sphere	Cube	Cone
Cylinder	Flat Rectangle	Wire	Wheels
Ring	Cross Bars	Block	Glue and Nails

Name: _____

Self-Assessment: Generating Ideas

Use the middle column to write your answers to each of the following questions. At a later date, re-assess your skill in generating ideas by completing the right hand column.

	Date:	Date:
1. List two of your best creative ideas that you have used.		
2. List two of your best creative ideas that you have not yet used.		
3. Finish this sentence: The best thing about ideas is…		
4. List your plan for improving the way you keep track of your ideas.		
5.a. What is an issue or subject or decision that you are working with right now? b. What's your perspective on it? c. What's a second perspective? d. A third perspective? e. Combine the three perspectives into one statement.		

CHAPTER 3

Asking Questions

Searching for Questions

3.01 Warm-up; 3.02 What Would You Like to Know?; 3.03 What Might Happen?; 3.04 How Can it Be Tested?; 3.05 Past, Present, and Future Searches; 3.06 Great Examples: Da Vinci's Questions

Searching for Solutions

3.07 Warm-up; 3.08 Discovering; 3.09 What's the Chance?; 3.10 The Road to Certainty; 3.11 Great Examples: Your Mind's Best Work

Reproducibles

Strategy Spot 3A: **What Are the Questions?**; Strategy Spot 3B: **Keep an Open Mind**; Quotes and Notes 3C: **Discovering**; Self-Assessment: **Asking Questions**

Asking questions is an important part of learning because it increases alertness and helps to connect information with prior knowledge and experience. Students can practise refining and focusing their questions so that they can identify what they would like to know and elicit more useful information. Skill in questioning is important in the fields of research, medicine, counseling, police work, marketing, and design. The related skill **hypothesizing** helps students to suggest possible solutions to a question based on present knowledge and experience.

Searching for Questions

3.01 Warm-up

Synopsis: Students practise generating questions.

Write the following headings on the board: Astronomy, Chemistry, World Peace, Mathematics, and Government. Ask students to record one question for each topic about something they are genuinely interested in knowing. Take a few minutes to share and compare questions. Ask: *How is asking questions important to your life? Why is it/isn't it important to find answers for all your questions? What questions do you have that you think will never be answered?*

Ask students to choose a picture from a book or magazine dealing with something they care about or are interested in. Have them reflect on the content of the picture and record questions they would like answered about it. They should be able to generate at least six or eight questions. Together, have students discuss and consider their questions.

To know how to wonder and question is the first step of the mind towards discovery.
Louis Pasteur

Supporting Learning: You may wish to post a sign on the class door: *What questions did you ask at school today?*

3.02 What Would You Like to Know?

Synopsis: Students create lists of their questions.

Ask: *What does a creative brain do for fun?* It takes a simple question and sees how many different ways there are of asking it. For example, if you ask, "Why is the sky blue?" are you really asking "Why isn't the sky orange?" or "How can the sky be different shades of blue?" or "What exactly do we mean by 'sky'?" Have students consider different ways of asking their questions.

Have students complete the following stem: *If I could learn anything at all, I would learn …*

Ask students to record ten questions that they would like answered about the natural world (animals, space, rocks, plants, and so on). They can use Strategy Spot 3A: **What Are the Questions?** to help them consider and develop their questions. Explain that using questions that begin with who, what, where, when, why, and how can elicit more information than questions beginning with is and are.

See also: 3.05 Past, Present, and Future Searches; 7.02: How Do You Word It?

Extension: Have students scan through resources in the classroom, looking for topics they would like to question, and for indications of what is unanswered in various fields. Students can start a list in a notebook or on a wall chart as they find more examples of the unanswered. Encourage students to share and compare their lists with their classmates.

Supporting Learning: Encourage students to ask questions that require more than a yes/no answer. Questions that begin with why, how, when, what, who, and where require answers with a deeper level of thought.

Science / Math Connection: Scientific education includes teaching students how to generate questions and to figure out how to answer them. And one of the best ways to spark the interest of students is to encourage them to learn about what is *not* understood in a subject as well as what is. Students may be interested in researching *The Seven Follies of Science* written by John Phin in 1906. These "unsolvable problems" include the perpetual motion machine, trisecting an angle, doubling a cube, squaring a circle, fixing mercury, turning lead into gold, and concocting an elixir of youth. There have been modern as well as ancient attempts at solving these problems. Small groups of students can research one of these problems to discover what progress has been made in each case. Have groups share their findings with the class.

3.03 What Might Happen?

Synopsis: Students practise making predictions.

Predicting involves using what you know to make an objective guess about the future. It may involve extrapolating beyond an observation or considering what happened before or after an event. One way of predicting is by exploring the laws that are involved in the event. Ask: *What do you predict will happen if we put water in the freezer?* (It will turn to ice.) *What do you predict will happen if I throw a ball up in the air?* (It will come back down.) These predictions are based on a familiarity with the laws governing movement of particles and gravity. Ask students for another example of a prediction based on a natural law.

Another way of predicting is by determining how likely a particular outcome is. Ask: *How likely is it that you would get more than 80% if we had a test on … today? What do you think will happen if we give this plant twice as much water?*

Ask students for another example of a prediction based on the likelihood of a particular outcome.

Students can predict what happened in the past as well as what might happen in the future. Ask students: *What is an example of a prediction you made for the future?* (I predicted my friend Mary would be at the movies and she was.) *What is an example of a prediction you made about the past?* (I predicted the reason I would not do well on the test was because I did not review the correct chapter.)

When the class is watching a video or as you are reading a book together, stop and have students predict what might happen next. On what are they basing their predictions? Suggest they make a habit of using commercial time to predict what will happen next on the TV shows they watch, and of taking breaks from reading to predict what will happen next, both in fiction and non-fiction sources.

Math Connection: Students might enjoy creating sequence puzzles for each other to solve. These could take the form of "Continue the pattern: 1, 4, 9, 16...." or "A, C, D, B, D, E,...

See also: 6.01 Warm-up

Science Connection: Ask students to imagine putting a puzzle together without a picture of the completed puzzle. Ask: *How might you approach this problem? What skills would you need to complete the puzzle?* Ask students to imagine one big box containing puzzle pieces from many different puzzles. Ask: *How would you know which pieces belonged to which puzzle? What skills would you need? How would you proceed?* Then discuss: *How is the puzzle analogy like scientific research and the skill of predicting?* You may wish to have students reflect on this question with a journal entry or in a three-paragraph essay format.

See also: 7.03 How Else Can You Think About It?

3.04 How Can it Be Tested?

Synopsis: Students form hypotheses about relationships they have noticed.

Ask students: *What is an hypothesis? What do you know about making hypotheses?* Hypotheses are suggested possible solutions to a problem based on present knowledge and experience, stated in a way that makes them testable. In other words, making an hypothesis is like making an educated guess. Students may be familiar with hypotheses from designing and performing investigations in science class. Have students recall (or research) some of the hypotheses they have worked with. Ask: *Does each hypothesis have all of these elements: a possible solution to a problem, based on present knowledge and understanding, and stated in a way that makes it testable?*

Ask: *When have you noticed patterns in natural events? When have you suspected a relationship that exists between certain events and outcomes?* Students might not be aware of how often they form hypotheses outside of science class. This might include the relationship between the number of hours of sleep they have and how well they do at school the next day, or the number of pieces of pizza they eat and how they feel afterwards. In each case, they have probably formed a hypothesis.

Have students work in pairs or small groups to make "If...then..." statements about patterns (e.g., "If the average overnight temperature goes below 0° C

Supporting Learning: Encourage students to use their predicting skills both in and out of the classroom. These skills can improve rapidly if they are practised. The point is not that the predictions have to be correct, but that the students develop liveliness in their awareness about what *might* happen next.

Though a theory might be Bohemian, it might be a parent of very respectable facts.
Sir Joseph John (J.J.) Thomson

Supporting Learning: Students may think that hypotheses are difficult or complicated. Reinforce that an hypothesis is basically making a guess about why something is the way it is, and that making a guess is a familiar skill to students. Have students record the guesses they make over the next few days, bring them to class, and work together to phrase them as hypotheses.

(32° F), then the water will freeze on the surface of the pond."). Then have students turn these statements into hypotheses (e.g., "The surface of the pond will freeze with an average overnight temperature of less than 0° C (32° F). Encourage students to word their hypotheses so that there is only one variable (a factor that could affect the outcome of an investigation or an event).

Challenge: Discuss the following quotation. Ask students: *Do you agree with this statement? Why, or why not?*

In fact any starting hypothesis may be fruitful if it leads to original calculations or new experiments. — *René Taton*

Have students reword a hypothesis so that it means the exact opposite, and challenge them to think about whether they might be able to find some supporting data for the new hypothesis. If not, the contradictory hypothesis is probably incorrect, and the original hypothesis is more likely to be correct. However, if some supporting data can be found for the contradictory hypothesis, it might be important to re-assess the original hypothesis. Encourage students to try this "contradictory" method with hypotheses they make in daily life as well as those in science class.

3.05 Past, Present, and Future Searches

Synopsis: Students consider past searches to plan a future search.

Ask students to describe what a science historian studies. Ask: *What might be learned from studying the scientific searches and methods used in the past?* One answer is that it might be possible to determine which results were obtained from good organization rather than chance. Another answer might be that the study could reveal patterns or trends in discoveries that might be applied to present-day and future searches. Ask students: *What value is there in learning about historical advances in science? What would you rank as the greatest scientific discovery of all time?* Record responses on a chart or on the board.

Have pairs of students design a "dream investigation" in which they would have all the materials, funding, and expertise to test any hypothesis. Ask: *What hypothesis would you choose, and why? What similar investigations in the past could you refer to?* Have students plan the investigation using scientific inquiry (identify the problem; describe how they would gather information; ask a question, form a hypothesis, and make a prediction; describe the steps of the investigation and how they might analyze the data). Remind students to word their hypothesis so that there is only one variable (one factor that could affect the outcome of an investigation).

See also: 3.02 What Would You Like to Know?; Strategy Spot 3A: **What Are the Questions?**; 3.08 Discovering; Strategy Spot 3B: **Keep an Open Mind**

Science Connection: Ask students: *What is more important in science: to gather more facts, or to better understand the facts already collected? Why?* Pairs of students with the same viewpoint can prepare an oral presentation of about 2-3 minutes about their reasons. They can share their responses with a small group, or with the whole class.

See also: 6.04 Patterns in Data

Career Connection: Discuss: *What skills would a science historian need? Which of those skills are similar to skills that a scientist needs? How might a person*

Who learns by finding out has seven fold the skill of him who learned by being told.
Arthur Guiterman

Supporting Learning: Less confident learners can join a small group where they will be able to help make predictions, suggest materials, and so on. Remind students to encourage all group members to contribute.

prepare for the career of science historian? Students can note which of the skills they have now would help them in the role of science historian.

3.06 Great Examples: Da Vinci's Questions

Synopsis: Students contribute answers to da Vinci's questions.

Ask: *What are some examples of questions that scientists might ask?* Record responses. Discuss the point that a scientist's questions are not necessarily complex or difficult. Leonardo da Vinci asked many questions about what he saw. Students might be able to answer some of the questions, either from prior knowledge or through researching. Ask students to work in small groups to answer the following paraphrased questions that da Vinci asked:

> Why are seashells found on the tops of mountains, along with imprints of plants that are usually found in the sea?
>
> Why does the light from lightning reach the eye before the sound of thunder reaches the ear?
>
> How does a bird hold itself in the air?

Students can share their answers with the class.

Searching for Solutions

3.07 Warm-up

Synopsis: Students consider the role of clear communication in asking and answering questions.

Ask students: *How would you rank your ability to give instructions? How would you rank your ability to follow instructions?* Students can use the following communication activity to refine their ability to ask clear questions and provide understandable answers. Working in pairs, have one student blindfolded or with eyes closed. Ask the "seeing" partner to use a colored pencil to draw a shape on a piece of paper marking an X at the beginning of the shape. (They should draw a relatively simple geometric shape at first, but as they practise they can make increasing complex designs.) Then the blindfolded partner can use a different colored pencil, and starting at the X, and follow the directions from the seeing partner to trace over the shape. The seeing partner can give all the directions needed, but cannot move the partner's hand or pencil. The blindfolded partner should keep the pencil on the paper at all times, but may ask questions to help guide the drawing. After each partner has had a turn, discuss how students can improve their ability to give directions and to ask questions that will elicit the information they need. Then they can draw a few more examples.

I roamed the countryside searching for answers to things I did not understand.
Leonardo da Vinci

Supporting Learning: If students have difficulty answering the questions, suggest they list questions that arise from their research or that they have about the same topic. Then share and discuss those questions.

It isn't answers that make a scientist, it's questions.
George Wald

Supporting Learning: Watch for improvement in students' questions and directions. Students may be confused with the use of "left" and "right" because they are sitting opposite each other. Suggest that each pair decide how to resolve that problem for themselves, and ask them to assess their methods after they are finished.

3.08 Discovering

Synopsis: Students consider the value of keeping an open mind.

Read or retell the following story to the class.

> A student visited a great master to learn about the truth of life. When he arrived the master poured him a cup of tea. The master poured the tea until it reached the brim of the cup and then he kept on pouring. The student was astonished and said, "My cup is full. No more can go in!" The master stopped pouring and smiled. "Exactly," he said. "Like this cup you are already full of your own ideas. How can I teach you anything new until you empty your cup?"

Discuss the story with students. Ask: *What did the master mean by "empty your cup"? What does it mean to have an open mind? In what ways is an open mind important in science? In art? In daily life?* Discuss times when students have changed their mind (opinion) based on new evidence or facts. Ask: *Why might we examine the beliefs, attitudes, and feelings that lie behind the choices we make?* You may wish to distribute and discuss Strategy Spot 3B: **Keep an Open Mind**, which presents several strategies for students to use when encountering new ideas.

Students can complete Quotes and Notes 3C: **Discovering** to consider and state their opinions regarding the act of discovery.

See also: 7.08 Breaking Assumptions

Language Arts/Social Studies Connection: Have students reflect on a discovery made by an explorer, artist, or researcher. Encourage students to visualize the events and imagine the feelings the discoverer had leading up to the discovery and then write a poem about the experience.

3.09 What's the Chance?

Synopsis: Students learn about techniques of increasing "chance" insights.

Ask students: *Have you ever had difficulty remembering information, such as a name, and then it popped into your mind later when you were doing something different? Describe what happened.*

Everyone has their own way of learning, remembering, creating, and questioning, but some techniques can be shared. Some creators like to increase the frequency of answers popping into their minds by learning all they can about the subject at hand. In fact, they "overload" the brain with information so that a maximum number of connections can be made and then they set it all aside and step into a fresh environment. Mathematician Henri Poincaré liked to purposefully "forget" the problems he was working on and be surprised by sudden insights about them when he was engaged in other activity. Thomas Edison would sometimes announce he had invented a device *before* he had invented it because the announcement demanded that he come through with the invention a short time later. Some creators find it useful to doodle, cluster, or play at certain points in the creating process.

Have students choose a family or community member to interview about their best techniques for getting ideas, and what they think the role that chance

---

The known is finite, the unknown is infinite; intellectually we stand on an island in the midst of an illimitable ocean of inexplicability. Our business in every generation is to reclaim a little more land.
T.H. Huxley

Supporting Learning: Spend time discussing the quotations so that students can be sure of the meaning of each quotation. Review Quotes and Notes 3C answers to observe that students give an opinion for each answer, and either a relevant example for "agree" answers, or a changed quotation and an explanation for "disagree" answers.

Chance favors the prepared mind.
Louis Pasteur

plays in their insights. Then they can pool their answers and search for patterns in the data.

See also: 2.03 Techniques of the Stars

Science/Technology/Career Connection: Simultaneous Discoveries. Ask: *What examples do you know of simultaneous or near-simultaneous discoveries?* (oxygen, the structure of DNA) Share the following quotation with students:

> . ... it seems to be true that many things have... an epoch in which they are discovered in several places simultaneously, just as the violets appear on all sides in the springtime.—*Wolfgang Bolyai*

What do students think might account for such a phenomenon? What might be the contribution of the almost-instant communication now available between parts of the world? Have students choose a career of interest to them and discuss the value of almost-instant, worldwide communication to the field.

3.10 The Road to Certainty

Synopsis: Students consider the role of mistakes and doubt in the creative process.

Ask students to think about these scenarios:

> ✓ *Imagine that you are painting a picture. You have the vision exactly right in your mind, but it is turning out differently when you try to paint it. What do you do?*
> ✓ *Suppose you accidentally drop a big splotch of paint on your paper. What do you do?*
> ✓ *What do you imagine a great artist would do when faced with a splotch of paint on paper?*
> ✓ *Does a great artist always know exactly what to do next to a painting? How does he or she decide?*
> ✓ *How often do you think a great scientist might say, "I don't know" or "I'm not sure?"*
> ✓ *How could a "mistake" turn into something helpful for a scientist?*

Ask students to think of a time in their own lives when something that seemed to be a mistake turned out to be helpful in getting them to think of a better idea. Mistakes, doubt, and uncertainty are parts of the lives of artists and scientists. Both work with the "unknown" and search for ways to find and express qualities hidden from view.

Students can work in pairs to invent slogans to remind themselves not to get frustrated with mistakes. Post the slogans around the classroom.

Science Connection: Have students consider this question: *Can any statement of scientific knowledge be absolutely certain? Why, or why not?* Ask students to support their answers with examples. They might gather in groups with other students who share the same view and together justify and present their reasons.

Supporting Learning: Students will benefit from writing their interview questions down. Encourage students to practice and refine their questions with a partner.

Next to being right in this world, the best of all things is to be clearly and definitely wrong because you will come out somewhere.
T.H. Huxley

Supporting Learning: ESL and other students can share examples of when a willingness to make mistakes (in pronunciation, etc.) helped them to learn or gain the information they needed. Encourage students to work with you in structuring an acceptance of "mistakes" in the classroom so that all the students are willing to contribute to discussions without fear of being "wrong."

3.11 Great Examples: Your Mind's Best Work

Synopsis: Students consider their best work conditions for searching for answers.

My mind seems to have become a kind of machine for grinding general laws out of large collections of facts.
Charles Darwin

Supporting Learning: Reinforce the concept that no particular learning style is better than another. Each has its strengths and weaknesses. Ask: *How is group work improved by having a variety of learning styles present?*

Charles Darwin admitted that he had a foggy memory, was a poor thinker, and could not easily grasp or abstract information. Because he realized his shortcomings, he was very careful when he collected data and recorded notes, and he methodically worked through problems. It was his careful attention that helped him to see the patterns that supported the theory of evolution. Some great creators (such as Mozart) worked quickly. Vincent Van Gogh could create a finished painting in two or three hours. Van Gogh would sometimes paraphrase American painter James McNeill Whistler and say that, *"It took me two hours to do the painting but forty years to learn how to do it in two hours."* Students can profile another great creator —themselves—by describing how, when, where, and under what conditions they work best when they are searching for answers. They can begin with the sentence stem "I work best when…"

Strategy Spot

What Are the Questions?

It has been said that it is better to use a big hook and not catch a big fish than to use a little hook and not catch a little fish. Go ahead and ask B-I-G questions to hook some B-I-G answers!

A. How to ask your questions

1. Use **WHO** when you want to identify individuals or groups who are part of your question, who might be able to provide information, or who might benefit from having the question answered. (Who is affected by it? Who created it? Who can help solve it?)

2. Use **WHAT** when you want to identify which things are included in the question, such as the outcomes, the causes and the effects, the advantages or disadvantages, the benefits, the applications, and so on. (What might happen next? What does this mean? What do I need to find out? What materials do I need?)

3. Use **WHERE** when you want to identify the focus of the question. (Where does it happen? Where else does this happen? Where did it begin? Where haven't I looked?)

4. Use **WHEN** to help you identify the time frame and order of events. (When did it start? When did the events occur? When will it finish?)

5. Use **WHY** when you want to understand the reasons for an action or outcome. (Why is this event occurring? Why is this observation significant? Why should this problem be solved?)

6. Use **HOW** when you want to identify the steps involved in a problem or solution. (How does it work? How can I get more objective information? How else can I look at the problem?)

B. How to think about your questions

Think about your questions in as many different ways as you can.

1. What do you want to find out?

2. What is the information you have? What is it you do not yet understand?

3. What can you figure out from the information you have?

4. What diagram, sketch, or cartoon of the question might help you?

5. What related questions or problems does your question remind you of?

6. How might you use the answer or method from a related problem to help you answer your question?

Worksheet 3A

Strategy Spot

Keep an Open Mind

When good scientists have an interesting idea, they do not decide whether they believe or disbelieve in the idea. They ask a question about it, formulate a hypothesis, and test the idea. Use the following strategies to help you keep an open mind when you encounter interesting ideas. Remember, the best scientists do not look for THE answer; they look for many answers.

1. **A good place to start is to recreate the research that led to a known discovery.**
   Question whether the conclusion seems correct and whether it might be reusable. When you repeat an investigation, be alert to notice what previous investigators might have overlooked. You might find something new about the procedure or results. See if you can find what has always been there but has gone unnoticed.

2. **Never assume that your idea has already been tested in quite the same way you want to test it**.
   Discovery is not just about finding something new, it is also about understanding what it means. Find the unique aspect of your results. Think about this quote by Alfred North Whitehead: "*Everything of importance has already been seen by someone who did not discover it.*"

3. **Keep in mind that a hypothesis can never be proven true.**
   A hypothesis can only be supported or rejected by the results of an investigation. In either case, you learn something. If an observation fits a hypothesis, then the hypothesis is supported, or reinforced. Repeat your investigation several (or more) times. Each time a hypothesis is tested and supported by data, it becomes more useful as an explanation.

4. **Consider denying evidence as well as confirming evidence.** The investigation is not a "failure" if the observations do not support the hypothesis. It simply means that the hypothesis needs to be revised and then tested. These steps of testing and revising are how knowledge advances and unexpected discoveries are made. Unexpected results can be a sort of treasure trove of information about your topic, an indication of where your research may lead you. The challenge is to figure out *why* the outcome was not what you expected.

5. **Be open to new directions or detours suggested by surprising observations or results.**
   What other aspects of your topic can you investigate to help you understand the data you have collected? What other ways are there of approaching and testing your original question?

Worksheet 3B

Name: _____

Discovering

For each quotation state whether you agree or disagree. If you agree, give an example of how this has been true in your own life. If you disagree, state why and change the statement to make it something you would agree with.

1. *I think that only daring speculation can lead us further and not accumulation of facts. — Albert Einstein*

   _____

   _____

   _____

2. *Discoveries are largely a function of the methods used. — Santiago Ramon y Cajal*

   _____

   _____

   _____

3. *Truth came out of error much more rapidly than it came out of confusion. — Francis Bacon*

   _____

   _____

   _____

4. *All creative scientists know that the true laboratory is in the mind, where behind illusions they uncover the laws of truth. — Sir Jagadis Chandra Bose*

   _____

   _____

   _____

5. *It is not the answer that enlightens, but the question. — Eugene Ionesco*

   _____

   _____

   _____

   _____

   _____

Worksheet 3C

Name: _____

Self-Assessment: Asking Questions

Use the middle column to write your answers to each of the following questions. At a later date, re-assess your skill in asking questions by completing the right hand column.

	Date:	Date:
1. How could you improve your skill in asking questions?		
2. Finish this sentence: The best questions…		
3. How could you improve your ability to make predictions?		
4. Finish this sentence: I would ask more questions if…		
5. How does asking questions help you in school? How does asking questions help you in your daily life?		
6. Finish this sentence: My best ideas come when…		

Connecting

The ability to make connections lies at the heart of creative and innovative thinking. Students can broaden their appreciation of the interconnectedness and interrelatedness of life by finding links among objects, ideas, and processes. Finding similarities among differences helps students to make and appreciate new combinations. Teachers, philosophers, artists, inventors, medical researchers, counselors, and architects call upon their connecting skills in everyday life. The related skill of **mapping** helps students to see connections through graphically representing a topic, issue, or subject.

Making Connections

4.01 Warm-up

Ideas awaken each other...because they have always been related.
Denis Diderot

Synopsis: Students find connections between random words.

Divide the class into small groups and give each group the same list of eight random nouns, such as grass, brick, toaster, cricket, penny, apple, and shovel. Have students divide the list into two groups using any method of grouping that they determine (e.g., number of syllables, double letters, things you find inside/outside). Then groups can present their lists and explain their method of grouping. What other categories did students consider? Discuss that our minds are incredible connection-making and connection-recognizing machines and that we can almost always find connections among different things. Ask: *When have you used your skill in finding connections between things?* (classifying, sorting, coding, comparing).

Supporting Learning: Students who find this activity easy could be challenged to find more unusual categories. Students who need more practice in generating categories for words may find it easier to work with manipulatives instead of words. Have them identify categories based on perceived qualities such as color, texture, size, weight, and so on.

Say not, 'I have found the truth,' but rather, 'I have found a truth.'
Kahlil Gibran

Supporting Learning: Suggest that students make a habit of keeping first drafts of their art and writing projects. Students can revisit the drafts as a source of ideas, or to appreciate how their skills have improved over time.

I begin to understand the foundations of a wonderful discovery ... All the sciences are interconnected as by a chain; no one of them can be completely grasped without taking the whole encyclopedia at once.
René Descartes

Groups can create a list of random nouns and exchange their lists with other groups to find connections.

4.02 Beyond Good and Bad

Synopsis: Students consider alternate categories for opinions.

List a number of words (or display some pictures) connected with foods (or other topics) that might elicit a strong reaction from students (such as ice cream, onions, mayonnaise, broccoli, hot peppers, zucchini). As you say or show each item, ask students whether they like or dislike it. Then discuss the limitations of using the categories "like/dislike." (How we categorize things can limit our ability to appreciate and make connections.) Ask: *What might be the benefit of reconsidering your choices? What new categories can you suggest to replace like/dislike?* (tried it/have not tried it; have seen the value/have not yet seen the value) Ask: *How might replacing the categories "good/bad" with something new affect how a scientist views an investigation or how an artist views a sculpture?*

Even the most familiar object can become fascinating if we consider new categories and new ways of viewing it. Have students suggest categories for viewing the objects in the room (material, origin, present use, possible future uses, its future if it is recycled, and so on.). They can work with a partner to complete a chart about common objects, using the categories suggested. Then discuss how this activity has increased their appreciation of the objects.

Art Connection: Encourage students to revisit art creations that they were dissatisfied with and consider how they could work further with the ideas they had. They can focus on what *did* work in the creation and what new directions are suggested.

4.03 A Class Act

Synopsis: Students discuss the value of connecting fields of learning.

Ask students to imagine a land in which there are many towers. One tower is where all the scientists work and live. Another tower is where all the artists live and create. Another tower is for the athletes. And so on. There is no communication among the towers. Ask students: *What would be the benefits of such a system? What might be the drawbacks?* Now have students imagine a land where the towers are divided by skill and experience. All the most skillful artists, scientists, athletes are in one tower. The less skillful are in another tower, and the least skillful are in another tower. There is no communication among the towers. Ask students: *What might be the benefits of such a system? What might be the drawbacks?* Then discuss: *Suppose there was another land that had not yet arranged people and towers. What would be the ideal way of arranging people and towers?* Discuss the importance of communication among fields of learning. Ask: *How do knowledge and advances in one field help encourage knowledge and advances in other fields?*

Have students think of an example of something they learned outside of class that connected to something they learned in school, or vice versa (e.g., learning how to calculate percentages in math class may have helped them calculate the new price at a "40% off" sale on shoes). Then have students complete Worksheet 4A: **Connect the Curriculum**, in which students make connections in their knowledge of two disciplines.

See also: 2.12 Abstractions (Challenge); 4.05 Great Examples: One Field Helps Another; 4.06 Warm-up; 9.06 The Whole Is Greater than the Sum of the Parts

Social Studies Connection: Students might consider how the tower scenario from this lesson can be applied to traditional factions, such as fans for one team versus fans for another team or people with opposing political views. Ask: *How might keeping the opposing factions apart affect the situation? What do you think would be the best arrangement? Why?*

Science Connection: Ask students: *If soft copper is added to even softer tin, then the resulting metal will be very soft, correct?* Have students support their predictions, and then tell them that Greek metallurgists were the first to discover that combining copper and tin produced bronze, a hard (not soft) alloy. Ask students: *What other alloys do you know? What different characteristics does the alloy have that the original elements did not have?*

Nature is an infinite sphere of which the center is everywhere and the circumference nowhere.
Blaise Pascal

Supporting Learning: Students will benefit from seeing examples of mind maps (such as your own) and realizing how much information can be condensed onto a map, and how free flowing the map can be. Discuss how this tool is useful in daily life for decision making, beginning a new project, and so on.

4.04 Maps of the Mind

Synopsis: Students use mind maps to connect and recall information.

One of the easiest ways to see connections is to literally see the connections by using a map to graphically represent a topic, issue, or subject. Ask: *What types of maps have you used to represent your ideas?* Discuss with students the benefits of mind maps (e.g., organize large amounts of information clearly, stimulate memory recall, represent connections visually, categorize information). Variations of mind maps include webs, clusters, concept maps, and so on. Discuss how a mind map shows the whole picture and the parts at the same time, making it easier to see where there are gaps in information. Distribute and discuss Strategy Spot 4B: **Make a Mind Map**, which leads students through the steps of creating a map of a subject.

Extension: Students can use mind maps to help them recall information for tests or exams. Ask students to choose something they would like to remember (e.g., information on a topic currently being studied). Then have them make a map of the information, including all the items to be remembered. Once it is complete, have students put it aside and take a fresh piece of paper and attempt to recreate the map from memory. When they think they are finished, they can compare it with the original map to note any differences. Encourage students to practise visualizing the map from time to time to keep it fresh in their minds. In a week's time, survey students to see how well they were able to recall this information. They may find it easier to remember a whole map than a list of facts.

See also: 1.08 Tips for Memorizing and Recalling

Synopsis: Students investigate how information from one field can help another.

Most people say that it is the intellect which makes a great scientist. They are wrong: it is the character.
Albert Einstein

Ask students to speculate how one discipline can contribute to a breakthrough in another discipline. Ask: *Suppose you were a biologist looking for a cure for a disease. What other disciplines (besides biology) might be helpful to your work?* (chemistry, physiology) *Suppose you were an astronomer. What other disciplines might be helpful to you?* (physics, geology) Many breakthroughs in science owe their basis to the integration of several disciplines. For example, Robert Bunsen, a nineteenth century chemist, casually mentioned to a physicist that he wanted to use color to determine elements, but hadn't found a satisfactory method. The physicist suggested using a prism to display the entire spectrum. That suggestion led to the science of spectrography and later to cosmology.

Supporting Learning: Encourage students to see that fields of learning are interconnected. Discuss why it is helpful for students to learn about many subjects while they are in grade school, rather than just whatever subject they like best. Ask: *How might it help you in your future career to know about a variety of subjects?*

Have students research examples where knowledge from one field led to progress, or a breakthrough, in another field. Students could research examples from their own lives, community leaders, or from history. If students research examples from their community, prepare students by having them carefully construct their questions in advance of interviewing their subjects. Students may prefer to present their findings using a flow chart or Venn diagram to show the contributions of the two fields and what was created when they were combined.

See also: 2.12 Abstractions (Challenge); 2.13 Great Examples: One Thing Leads to Another; 4.03 A Class Act; 4.06 Warm-up

Career Connection: Some scientists are also musicians. Some artists are also athletes. Some teachers are also poets. Some doctors are also dancers. Ask students: *How might musical or artistic involvement help to make a better scientist? How might scientific training help to make a better poet? What type of occupations might require a person to develop both artistic and scientific expertise?* Students can consider that character, upbringing, emotions, experiences, philosophy, and many other factors help to shape personality and perceptions, as does formation of ideas, motives, and attitudes.

See also: 2.12 Abstractions (Challenge); 4.03 A Class Act; 4.06 Warm-up

Thinking Is Linking

4.06 Warm-up

Synopsis: Students consider the role of unusual connections.

The test of a first-rate intelligence is the ability to hold two opposed ideas in the mind at the same time, and still retain the ability to function.
F. Scott Fitzgerald

Ask students: *What do you get when you cross a calculator with an athletic shoe?* (a shoe that calculates how far it has gone? a calculator that "runs" on movement?) Have students describe the process of thinking they went through to find their answers. They may have spent a few seconds (or more) wondering about the question and to connect two such different objects. When they thought of an answer they liked, they may have had the experience of "I know!" or "Aha!"

Discuss: *An inventive mind can generate many connections between dissimilar objects.* For example, Samuel Morse was trying to devise a way to send radio signals over great distances. One day he saw tired horses being exchanged for fresh ones at a relay station and made the connection of having relay stations for boosting radio signals over great distances. This connection made coast-to-coast telegraph possible. Morse used an ordinary concept (exchanging horses) and applied it in a new and different way to inspire a breakthrough in thinking.

An inventor's insights have more to do with the processing of information (*how* to think) than with the amount of information available (*what* to think). Ask: *What other examples of unusual connections do you know, either from your own life, or from others'? The connections could be direct (physically connecting the forms of things) or indirect (conceptually connecting the processes of things).* Discuss: *The more connections one makes, the more likely is the chance of an original idea.*

Students can complete Worksheet 4C: **Think and Link** in which they practise finding links between words to create sentences.

See also: 2.12 Abstractions, 4.03 A Class Act; 4.05 Great Examples: One Field Helps Another

Language Arts Connection: Have students find figures of speech in literature (especially similes, metaphors, and personification) and analyze what things or processes are being connected in each instance (e.g., simile: "The ocean is like a cat pouncing on the shore." ocean-cat; metaphor: "She had a heart of stone." heart-stone; personification: "The storm marched across the field." storm- soldier). Ask: *Which do you find the most effective? Why?*

4.07 Combinatory Play

Synopsis: Students play with words and connections.

In *The Act of Creation,* Arthur Koestler explains creative thinking as a process of 'bisociation,' the perception of something in two different frames of reference which have something, but not all, in common. An example is a pun. Ask students: *What is a pun? What are your favorite puns?* Together, analyze what is held in common in the examples of puns that students provide. (e.g., "Once you've seen one shopping center you've seen a mall." "A mall" takes the place of "them all" in the common saying "you've seen them all.") Have students create puns combining pun and fun/funny. (e.g., Now that's punny! Just for the pun of it.)

Another way to look at the principle of bisociation is to *unconnect* – take two words that are very closely related and find something different about them. Have students complete Worksheet 4D: **Uncrossed Word Puzzle**, in which students identify words with different meanings and pronunciations that have the same spelling. (**Answers: Across** 3. sewer 4. number 5. close 6. tear 8. polish 9. does 10. wound 12. lead 13. desert **Down** 1. present 2. object 3. subject 7. refuse 8. produce 10. wind 11. dove) Students can create their own "uncrossed word puzzles" for each other to solve.

See also: 2.10 Playing with Ideas; any of the collections of mathematical puzzles by Martin Gardner.

Math Connection: Students could play Math Connection in which one student writes an equation, such as 23 + 22 = 45, and the next student uses the last number to start the next equation (45 = 9 x 5). Make the game more difficult by limiting the choice of numbers or operations.

Supporting Learning: Check that students' sentences for Worksheet 4C make sense. If students have difficulty with this activity, suggest they use several sentences instead of just one.

When a thing is funny, search it carefully for a hidden truth.
George Bernard Shaw

Supporting Learning: Before completing Worksheet 4D, students may find it useful to discuss words that have the same spelling but different meanings. (sink, rose, time, run, bass) You might also discuss how some words can be used as nouns or verbs.

Social Studies Connection: Students could play Geography Connection, in which one student names a country (or other category chosen in advance, such as cities or rivers) and the next student names another that starts with the last letter of the first country (e.g., Egypt, Taiwan, New Zealand). Carry on as long as possible without using any countries twice.

4.08 Connectability

Synopsis: Students make connections between words and ideas.

A wonderful harmony is created when we join together the seemingly unconnected.
Heraclitus

Supporting Learning: Encourage group members to make sure all members have a chance to contribute ideas and are part of the decision-making process.

Supporting Learning: If students are unsure about where to begin without a topic, encourage them to choose pictures based on what they like, or what makes them stop and look more closely. Then after they have collected a few pictures and headlines they can try putting them together and see what is a common theme.

Write the words "dog" and "cat" on the board. What connections can students name between the two pets? (both are mammals, four-legged) After a few suggestions, ask: *How can you turn a dog into a cat?* The answer is by changing one word into another, one letter at a time (e.g., dog →dot →cot →cat). Ask students to figure out some other ways of getting from "dog" to "cat" (e.g., dog →cog →cot →cat). Students can practise making up their own examples of word connections for a partner to see how few transitions they need to get from one word to the other word. Students may find it easier if they start with words of one syllable (such as lose— find; lamp—tile; milk—fine; near—rent).

Students could play *Connect This!* Divide the class into several groups. Choose a topic, such as a current discussion at school (e.g., "How can students get better grades?") or a community issue ("How could we design a skate park?"). Ask each group to record an *unrelated* idea (have live music at our dances) or *impractical* suggestion (let the students run the school). Then each group exchanges their unrelated ideas with another group. Give groups three minutes to turn the unrelated idea into a practical solution for the original question (e.g., Design a skate park that has a stage so that live bands can play there. The students who raise their grades the most are given an afternoon to "shadow" the principal or a teacher and help make decisions.) Repeat several times, using the same issue or a new issue. Discuss what students found easy, difficult, or surprising about the game.

Extension: Have students randomly cut out images, words, and headlines that interest them from a variety of magazines. Ask students to make a collage with the cuttings; however, do not assign a topic for the collage. At first, students may not be sure of what kind of collage they will make, but eventually the moment will come when they know what they want to say and then they will find the materials they need for their collages. Have students present their collages and discuss the process they went through to decide the collage's subject and to determine which elements to include. Ask: *How did you decide what the collage would be about? At what stage did you make your decision?*

4.09 Are Two Doctors a Paradox?

Synopsis: Students consider how paradoxes stimulate creative thinking.

A paradox is a statement that contradicts itself, or suggests logical arguments that can lead to an incorrect conclusion. For example, a paradox from the 6th century states: *Epiminides, a Cretan, says all Cretans are liars.* (If Epiminides is a Cretan and all Cretans are liars, then Epiminides is lying when he says all Cretans are liars.) Some common modern paradoxes include:

Please ignore this statement. – *Editor*

There are no errors in this book except this one. – *Editor*

Ask students what they know about paradoxes and how they first heard of them. Discuss the three paradoxes mentioned above. Ask: *What makes each one a paradox? How might a paradox stimulate the mind to think creatively?* (challenge assumptions; challenge the mind to find how two opposing concepts can be reconciled through connections) Read students the following statement by a Nobel Prize winner.

How wonderful that we have met with paradox. Now we have some hope of making progress. –*Niels Bohr*

Ask students what they think Bohr meant by this statement. (Paradoxes can inspire a new way of thinking or an intellectual breakthrough.)

Distribute and discuss Worksheet 4E: **Zeno's Paradox** and/or Quotes and Notes 4F: **Paradoxically Speaking**, both of which ask students to consider and respond to famous paradoxes. (**Answer:** The mistaken assumption in Zeno's paradox is that an infinite number of progressively decreasing time steps will add up to an infinite time interval. Achilles will, of course, pass the tortoise and win the race. **Note:** Although paradoxes are sometimes dismissed out-of-hand, they can lead to important discoveries. If Zeno's paradoxes had been more seriously considered in his day, it may be that calculus would have been developed much sooner.)

Extension: Students can research the "Hotel Infinity" paradox (for example, www.c3.lanl.gov/mega-math/workbk/infinity/infinity.html). They can use a flow chart or other graphic representation to explain the paradox.

Math Connection: Have students plan how to research examples of other paradoxes in mathematics (including several more by Zeno, Bertrand Russell's paradox, Cantor's infinities). Once students establish a plan, have them share their plans with you for consideration before starting the research.

See also: Strategy Spot 7D: **Working Through a Problem**

Science Connection: Can disease function to prevent disease? That was the paradox that Louis Pasteur found himself considering when several infected chickens survived a cholera bacillus. That paradox led to the discovery of the principle of immunology. Discuss other examples of paradoxes that led to a breakthrough in science. Another example is based on Aristotle's declaration that a heavier body falls faster than a lighter body. Galileo considered that therefore two gold coins would fall at the same rate because they are equally heavy. But suppose the coins are joined by a light thread. According to Aristotle the coins should now fall faster. The speed cannot increase, since neither coin can pull the other down faster. After thinking about this paradox, Galileo

Supporting Learning: Some students may benefit from working in a small group with you, illustrating Worksheet 4E together, and discussing each of the paradoxes on Worksheet 4F before working independently.

concluded that Aristotle was wrong, and that all bodies must fall at the same rate in the absence of air resistance. This breakthrough made it possible for Sir Isaac Newton to later discover the laws of motion. Other examples of paradoxes can be found in Albert Einstein's work with reference frames and the laws of physics, and Heinrich Olbers' questioning of why the sky is dark at night. Have students research the examples discussed or their own examples that they discover through research.

Language Arts Connection: There are many examples of paradoxes within the use of the English language. For example, a fat chance and a slim chance mean the same thing, an alarm goes off by going on, a house burns up as it burns down, an application form is filled in by being filled out, and a boxing ring is square. Students could work in small groups to name other paradoxes and contradictions in the English language.

4.10 Great Examples: Connect and Create

Synopsis: Students consider inventions made by connecting and creating.

How many of the following inventions can students name? Have students work together in pairs to research and answer the questions. If time allows, have students research and create their own "Connect and Create" questions to exchange with another pair.

The ability to relate and to connect sometimes in odd and yet striking fashion, lies at the heart of any creative use of the mind, no matter in what field or discipline.
George J. Seidel

Connect and Create Questions

James Watt connected steam and transportation to invent…?
(high-pressured steam engine)

William Harvey connected a water pump and the human heart to develop…?
(modern theory of circulation)

Charles Darwin connected random genetic mutations and natural selection to develop…?
(theory of evolution)

Johann Gutenberg connected a grape press and a coin punch to make…?
(printing press)

Arthur Frye connected a bookmark and temporary glue to create…?
(Post-it notes)

Name: _____

Connect the Curriculum

There are many connections among all the subjects you study in school. For example, learning about fractions in math makes it easier to convert recipes in a cooking class, or measure where to cut a block of wood in a woodworking class, or analyze a survey in Social Studies. For each of the following subjects, name something you have learned in the first subject that connects with something you have learned in the second subject.

1. Science ➜ Social Studies

_____

_____

2. Science ➜ Language Arts

_____

_____

3. Language Arts ➜ Social Studies

_____

_____

4. Math ➜ Science

_____

_____

5. Math ➜ Social Studies

_____

_____

6. Language Arts ➜ Math

_____

_____

7. Any of the Fine Arts (music, drama, art, etc.) ➜ Science

_____

_____

8. Any of the Fine Arts ➜ Math

_____

_____

Make a Mind Map

Mapping is one way to find out what you know, think, and feel about a subject. Before you begin studying a new subject or topic, make a mind map. Here's how to do it:

1. **Print your topic, question, or challenge in the center of the page.** Use colors or draw a diagram.

2. **Print thoughts, feelings, and other associations like vines growing out from the center.** Add whatever thoughts come to mind, without judging or evaluating. Fill up the page as quickly as you can.

3. **Use a variety of colors and arrows.** Develop a personal style, but keep your printing fairly upright so you can easily read it later. Anything goes: leave blanks, ask questions, add more vines growing from other vines. Keep adding whatever comes to mind.

4. **After mapping, ask yourself:**
   How did mapping add to my understanding of the topic? What did I find out that I didn't consider earlier? What areas are unclear or need more developing? Which ideas can be "weeded out"? Which ideas shall I explore further?

5. **Consider your map a "work in progress."** Revise it from time to time as you learn more about your subject. As you revise your map, you'll begin to notice that major themes and ideas evolve.

6. **Variation.** Decide and list the major themes of your subject. Ask yourself: If my subject were a book, what would be its title, subtitle, and chapter titles? Then create a map, starting with the title in the center, for each of the titles you identified.

Worksheet 4B

Name: _____

Think and Link

How can you get from one word to the next? Choose any three words at random and link them together in a sentence. For example, "Looking out my *window*, I could see the *clouds* forming above the *volcano*." Then use four random words. For an extra challenge, use all the words contained in one row in a sentence. You can choose the same row as a partner and then compare your sentences.

dictionary	clouds	volcano	octopus	triangle
poster	milk	horse	drum	fog
ice	glue	telephone	sky	notebook
ocean	book	stamp	paint	needle
field	motor	window	road	zoo
butter	umbrella	shoe	cup	gate
mattress	fossil	rose	insect	soup
envelope	bench	magnet	tent	planet
library	tomato	flag	worm	key
circus	ladder	calendar	rainbow	orchestra
bread	chalk	ballet	spoon	child
cabin	bone	syrup	jungle	crayons
kite	zipper	tractor	garden	paper
sweater	floor	barn	dolphin	glove
battery	bagel	box	lemon	lightning

Name: _____

Uncrossed Word Puzzle

In this puzzle you can practise using your ability to make connections. Two clues are given for each word. The answers to both clues are spelled the same, but have a different meaning and pronunciation. Good luck connecting the clues!

Clues

Across

3. a person who sews; a sewage drain
4. to feel less sensation; examples are 1, 3, and 7
5. near to; opposite of open
6. comes when you cry; comes when you rip
8. from Poland; to shine
9. several female deer; present tense of did
10. a cut; past tense of wind
12. to be out front; an element
13. to leave; a hot dry sandy place

Down

1. to give to; in attendance
2. to disagree; another name for a thing
3. a course of study; under the power of
7. garbage; opposite of accept
8. to make; fruits and vegetables
10. movement of air: to wrap around
11. a type of pigeon; past tense of dive

Worksheet 4D

Name: _____

Zeno's Paradox

Zeno was a Greek philosopher who lived about 2500 years ago. He is famous for several paradoxes. One of his paradoxes is about a race between a young athlete and a tortoise. Read the paradox and see if you can solve the problem so that Achilles can win the race. Draw an illustration of each part of the story as you read.

Illustrations

1. The crowd cheers wildly as Achilles and the tortoise step up to the starting line. Achilles knows he can run twice as fast as the tortoise, so to make the race fair, he gives the tortoise a head start of exactly half the length of the race.

_____

2. The race begins, and Achilles runs to the place where the tortoise began. But by the time he reaches the place the tortoise has traveled half of the distance from its starting place to the finish line.

_____

3. Achilles runs to the tortoise's new position. But by the time he reaches it, the tortoise has traveled half the distance remaining between that spot and the finish line.

_____

4. Every time Achilles runs to the next spot, the tortoise has already traveled half the remaining distance, so Achilles is never able to catch the tortoise.

_____

What is wrong with the logic in this story?

_____

_____

_____

_____

Worksheet 4E

Quotes and Notes

Paradoxically Speaking...

Read the following paradoxes and choose your favorite. Turn it into a graphic representation, such as a banner, bumper sticker, or poster.

Not every thing that counts is countable and not every thing that is countable counts.
Albert Einstein

The way up and the way down are the same.
Heraclitus

The people sensible enough to give good advice are usually sensible enough to give none.
Eden Phillpotts

A man who fears suffering is already suffering from what he fears.

Michel Eyquem de Montaigne

A physicist is an atom's way of knowing about atoms.
George Wald

The only wealth which you will keep forever is the wealth which you have given away.
Marcus Valerius Martial

Every exit is an entry somewhere else.
Tom Stoppard

It is in giving that we receive, it is in pardoning that we are pardoned.
St. Francis

Real knowledge is knowing the extent of one's ignorance.
Confucius

Where there is a great deal of light, the shadows are deeper.
Johann Wolfgang von Goethe

Worksheet 4F

Name: _____

Self-Assessment: Connecting

Use the middle column to write your answers to each of the following questions. At a later date, re-assess your skill in connecting by completing the right hand column.

	Date:	Date:
1. What is your plan for improving your ability to make connections?		
2. Finish this sentence: The more connections I make…		
3. Finish this sentence: One piece of information that I can connect to many parts of my life is…		
4. Finish this sentence: I can use maps to…		
5. How does your ability to make connections help you in your schoolwork?		
6. How does your ability to make connections help you in your daily life?		

CHAPTER 5

Making Analogies

> **What Does This Remind You Of?**
>
> 5.01 Warm-up; 5.02 A Close-up Look at Analogies 5.03 It's Like This; 5.04 Personal Analogies; 5.05 Great Examples: Shapes and Forms
>
> **Making Familiar Things New**
>
> 5.06 Warm-up; 5.07 Name It! 5.08 What Might Be; 5.09 Limits of Analogies 5.10 Great Examples: Biomimicry
>
> **Reproducibles**
>
> Worksheet 5A: **This Reminds Me**; Worksheet 5B: **It's Like This!**; Worksheet 5C: **Make a Koch Curve**; Self-Assessment: **Making Analogies**

An analogy is a comparison between two dissimilar objects, ideas, or processes that have some qualities in common. Often, analogies explain the unfamiliar by using the familiar, such as when a camera is compared to an eye. Analogies are an essential part of creativity because they provide the conceptual basis for theories and ideas by identifying relationships between things that cannot be explicitly compared or literally equated. Students can expand their thinking by using analogies to find and consider relationships. Poets, visual artists, inventors, scientists, mathematicians, and humorists make regular use of analogies in their work. The related skill of **naming** helps students to notice details in appearance, function, location, and so on.

What Does This Remind You Of?

5.01 Warm-up

Synopsis: Students learn how to construct analogies.

The chessboard is the world, the pieces are the phenomena of the universe, the rules of the game are what we call the laws of nature.
T.H. Huxley

Hold up an orange and a ball (or two other similar objects) and ask students: *How is an orange like a ball? What else is an orange like? Why?* Then encourage students to go beyond naming similarities of color or form by asking: *How is an orange like a smile?* (they are both sweet) *How is the taste of an orange like a swim on a hot day?* (they are both refreshing) Explain that an analogy helps you see what one thing is like by comparing it with something else. You may wish to discuss the analogy in the margin quotation by T.H. Huxley.

One way of constructing analogies is to use the following format in which parts of the statement are based on identifying the same function or relationship. *Earth is to the Sun as the Moon is to ….. (Earth).*

In this case the relationship is which orbits which. Have students create some analogy puzzles for each other to solve (A clock is to time as a scale is to...Up is to down as in is to ...)

5.02 A Close-up Look at Analogies

Synopsis: Students find resemblances in magnified objects.

Display some pictures of objects that have been magnified many times. (Children's science magazines sometimes feature such pictures for readers to guess the object.) Or you can provide magnifying glasses or loupes for students to view real phenomena (rocks, leaves, moss, sugar, wood). For each object ask students: *What does this remind you of?* Tell students that the point of this activity is not to guess what they are seeing, but just to look for similarities to other objects. List students' responses and encourage them to brainstorm other resemblances. For each response, ask: *Why does it remind you of that?* Then reveal what the object is and have students revisit the items on the list, determining analogies between the object and the listed items. Discuss how the difference in scale changes the successfulness of the analogies.

You may wish to have students complete Worksheet 5A: **This Reminds Me**, in which they find resemblances between simple figures and other objects, and create simple figures for a partner to examine. Students can use the list of analogies from this lesson as starting points for poems, illustrations, research projects, inventions, and so on.

See also: 2.09 Warm-up; The Private Eye program, which was piloted in Seattle schools, suggests numerous analogy exercises using a magnifying loupe. See www.the-private-eye-project.com

5.03 It's Like This

Synopsis: Students use a variety of ways to express an analogy.

Ask students: *How is the mind like a garden?* (All sorts of ideas blossom and grow if they are "watered.") *What else is the mind like? Why?* Brainstorm a number of analogies and record responses. Then ask students to use one of these analogies to develop each of the following: a) write a figure of speech, such as a simile or metaphor (For an ocean analogy: A thought is like a wave on an ocean.) b) develop a story outline a few sentences long (For a jungle analogy: They searched through the dense jungle of thoughts hoping to find the elusive answer to their question. Their trail took them into regions they had only suspected existed.) c) form a hypothesis (For a mine analogy: The best thoughts are hidden deep within the mind.) d) create a joke (What do you want to do at the end of a busy day? Relax and unmind.) and e) make a drawing (For a tree analogy: labeling the root of thought and the fruit of thought.)

After students complete and discuss this activity, they might enjoy playing the game in Worksheet 5B: **It's Like This!**, which has students create analogies to compare two different objects.

See also: Worksheet 8A: **Transform Your Knowledge**

Challenge: Have students make analogies and create visual representations for connections between science and art; the universe and the brain; the Earth

Supporting Learning: If students need more practice in finding resemblances, collect their drawings from Worksheet 5A and make a worksheet with some of the sketches. Use some of the other sketches to work through as a class.

Supporting Learning: Depending on the level of your students, you may wish to work through this activity as a class.

and a cell; or knowledge and experience (e.g., "Science is like art because it searches for ways to describe finer levels of creation." The visual representation could be a drawing of an artist and scientist side by side, the artist with a brush, the scientist with a microscope, both exclaiming, "At last I see the finer levels!")

Science Connection: Many scientists rate analogizing as one of their most important mental skills. Ask students to suggest reasons why this might be so. (Analogies help scientists investigate phenomena that are too big, too small, too fast, etc. to be directly observed.)

Language Arts Connection: William Wordsworth wrote of *"the pleasure the mind derives from the perception of similitude in dissimilitude."* Ask students to reflect on his statement and respond with a journal entry. Prompt students' thinking by asking: *What do you think this means? What similar experience have you had in your own life?*

Math/Art Connection: Show students some pictures of fractals and ask what they remind them of. Record responses. Then ask students what they know about fractals, and how they would define a fractal based on the pictures they have seen. (A fractal is an irregular shape in which a part is similar in shape to a larger part and a smaller part if it is magnified or reduced to the same size.) Have students complete Worksheet 5C: **Make a Koch Curve** (or simply read them the directions and let them discover what shape is made). Ask: *What does the Koch curve remind you of?* Students may wish to investigate other fractals, such as Hilbert Curves, and Torn Squares.

See also: Worksheet 6C: **Make a Sierpinski Carpet;** 8.04 Making Models; 9.05 Warm-up

5.04 Personal Analogies

Synopsis: Students learn about personal analogies.

…there is an inexhaustible ocean of likenesses between the world within and the world without…
Helen Keller

Write this question on the board: *How can we learn about or explain anything that we cannot directly perceive? What examples can you think of?* Ask students to reflect and suggest some answers, or to comment on the question. Then ask students to share what they know about Helen Keller. Ask: *How could a person who could not see or hear learn anything about the world of the seeing and hearing?* Helen Keller spoke of trying to bridge the gap between the eye and the hand through using personal analogies. A "personal analogy" involves putting oneself imaginatively inside a problem, or in other words, how a person explains events, objects, or phenomena to him- or herself. Helen Keller likened the freshness of a flower in her hand to the taste of a just-picked apple. She compared the variety of fragrances that she enjoyed to how the eye might be charmed by a variety of colors. Students could research other analogies that Keller used.

Ask students: *What are your personal analogies for perceiving the world?* To prompt students, have them complete the following stem:

Life is like a… (bowl of cherries, box of chocolates, a grocery store).

Supporting Learning: Some students may benefit from discussing the suggested analogies before making their collage.

Write student responses on the board. Have students represent their personal analogies in a collage or other representation. They should include a caption that explains their analogy.

See also: 9.02 Linking Physical Senses

Language Arts Connection: Students may have some familiarity in recognizing similes and metaphors in literature. Ask them to name some of their favorite examples (or ask them to record some favorites and bring them to class to share). Remind them to note the source of each. Ask students to choose one of the similes or metaphors to use as the basis for writing a poem that shows how it applies to their life. Alternately, use the title of a poem (such as Robert Frost's "Nothing Gold Can Stay") and ask students to brainstorm all the different things/experiences it might refer to. Then ask them to write a poem using the same title to explore one of the items from the brainstormed list.

Science Connection: Chemist Primo Levi used the qualities of the elements as analogies for experiences in his own life. You may wish to read a section of his book, *The Periodic Table,* to students and have students make similar analogies between the elements and their own lives.

Math Connection: Stanislaw Ulam stated that a good mathematician is one who finds analogies between things; a great mathematician is one who finds analogies between analogies. Discuss the use of analogies in Math. Ask: *How have you used analogies to understand mathematical concepts?* You might like to discuss an analogy such as the following to encourage students' willingness to explore mathematical concepts: Ask: *How is solving a problem in math similar to this scenario? If you are in a hurry to walk to school you might miss many details in the scenes you pass. But if you have more time, you may notice more of your surroundings, or may explore different ways to get to school.* (If you search for an answer in mathematics thinking there is only one right way, or one right answer, you are like the person going straight to school. But instead you can think like an explorer, "The answer is here somewhere. If I keep looking I'll find it.")

Career Connection: People often use analogies in their jobs. For example, doctors often use analogies to help explain an illness to a patient (e.g., "Think of your body as a machine. It needs an occasional tune-up to keep it running smoothly.") Have students choose an occupation and interview a member of it to discover how he or she uses analogies at work. Post the results on a class bulletin board.

5.05 Great Examples: Shapes and Forms

Synopsis: Students look for analogous forms.

Ask students: *What does an airplane remind you of? What do its wings remind you of? What does a helicopter remind you of? What does its propeller remind you of?* Discuss: *Analogies can help to reframe a problem and find an unexpected solution.* For example, the technology of flight was developed, in part, through the use of analogies. When Leonardo da Vinci considered flight, he considered a propeller as being an air screw. The propeller "holds on" to air much as a wood screw holds on to wood. From his early analogy the helicopter was later developed. When the Wright brothers considered propellers, they likened them to rotary wings. From that analogy, aircraft propellers were developed.

Students can "work backwards" by selecting an invention and predicting one or more analogies that might have been useful in its development. Have students post labeled illustrations of their analogies and inventions.

Nature is an artist that works from within instead of from without.
John Dewey

Supporting Learning: Encourage students to predict by letting them know there are no "right" or "wrong" answers, though students should be able to explain how the invention could have evolved from their choice of analogies.

Making Familiar Things New

5.06 Warm-up

Synopsis: Students use an analogy to teach a partner.

Supporting Learning: If students are uncomfortable or unable to teach another student, they could scan through a science or other textbook and list analogies. A good topic is atomic models, in which atomic structure has been compared through time to billiard balls, plum pudding, the solar system, and a cloud.

Ask students: *What examples of analogies can you recall from a subject in school? What analogies have you heard a teacher use or have read in a textbook?* When there is new knowledge to assimilate or understand there is often something familiar and at hand that it can be connected to. For example, a student may not be familiar with how the heart functions, but may understand how a pump functions. Have students choose some knowledge that they have that a classmate might not have (such as how to play a musical instrument, or control a certain computer function, or use a type of equipment, etc.) Students can create and use an analogy to teach a partner about the topic. Afterwards, have partners discuss how effective the analogies were in helping them understand.

5.07 Name It!

Synopsis: Students create names based on resemblances.

Write on the board: "horseless carriages" and "iron horses." Ask students: *Do you know what early inventions these names represent?* (automobiles and trains) *Why do both names use the word "horse" even though an automobile and a train do not look like a horse?* (It helped people understand the unfamiliar by relating it to something familiar; Automobiles and trains replaced the function of horses.) Ask: *In what ways can names be helpful to perception? In what ways can names be limiting to perception?* For example, the word *atom* means "indivisible" in Greek, and for many hundreds of years it was assumed that therefore the atom *was* indivisible. (You may wish to discuss the margin quotation by Thomas Hobbes.) Ask students to suggest what possibilities might be opened or closed by the name "computer mouse."

Supporting Learning: Some students may benefit from being paired with a partner with more advanced language skills.

The process of naming something encourages a person to notice the details of the object being named. The following activity can be done inside or outside. Establish a time limit (10 or 15 minutes) and ask each student to find and name a certain number (5-10) of objects (you might wish to specify living or non-living). Students can make up names based on appearance, function, location, or needs. (If they know the correct name of the object, tell them to ignore it and make up their own name.) Then, in pairs, students can compare names for the same objects, or exchange their list of names and try to identify the objects based on the names.

See also: 5.08 What Might Be

Social Studies Connection: Students can suggest new names for towns, cities, and countries based on the geography of the area. They could also research unusual names of places and discover how and why the names were chosen.

Math Connection: Mathematician Henri Poincaré once stated that mathematics is the art of giving the same name to different things. Ask students to consider what he might have meant by this and to suggest examples that support or refute his statement.

5.08 What Might Be

Synopsis: Students consider alternate uses for common objects.

Ask students: *When have you used a tool or other object for a purpose other than its intended use?* Record responses and discuss the analogies that were used. (e.g., using a book to prop open a window. How is a book like a wedge? If a wedge works a certain way, then why not a book?)

Ask students to share experiences they have had similar to the following: When a child is given a new toy, he or she might explore different ways of playing with the toy — pounding it on the ground, rolling it, etc., and might even overlook the use for which it was intended. Or a child might take an object that is not a toy and use it to play with (brooms used as horses, large cardboard boxes used as houses or cars). Discuss: *Discoveries arise from the ability to see objects for their potentiality rather than trying to label and categorize them.*

Have students work in pairs to brainstorm alternate uses for several everyday objects, such as a brick, fork, and pencil. They can name their inventions and compare lists when they are finished.

See also: 5.07 Name It! 7.09 Sources for Inventions

Technology Connection: Students can consider the different analogizing possibilities of different toys such as video games and wooden blocks. (Wooden blocks offer more possibilities of analogizing because they can represent so many different things.) Ask: *When might it be important for a toy to have more analogy possibilities? When might it be less important?*

5.09 Limits of Analogies

Synopsis: Students investigate the limits of an anology's usefulness.

Ask students: *In what ways is Earth like a cell?* Record responses. Then discuss the fact that analogies have limits to their usefulness. For example, Earth isn't really like a cell, even though comparing the two reveals similar or shared properties. Ask: *What are some important ways in which Earth is not like a cell?* Record responses. Discuss: *When using analogies, one needs to be aware of what its limits are and which different analogies can be used to think about the relationships between the same objects.* Ask: *What else can Earth be compared to?*

Students may be interested in learning an example of an inaccurate analogy in René Laënnec's invention of the stethoscope in 1816. Laënnec recalled that if you place your ear against one end of a wooden beam, the scratch of a pin at the other end is very distinct. Thinking that wood makes sound more audible, he rolled a piece of paper, placed one end over his patient's chest, placed his ear at the other end, and was able to hear the heart much more distinctly. However, it was not a quality of wood or paper that allowed him to hear the heartbeat, it was that the hollow tube focused and reflected the sound better. His analogy, although useful, was incorrect.

Discuss: *Skill in analogical thinking demands not only selecting the right model for comparison, but also understanding the limits of the analogy. An analogy is sometimes only valid for understanding part of a process, and cannot be applied to the process as a whole.* Have students work in pairs to consider any analogy they wish and identify at what point it breaks down or is no longer useful (the limit

---

Make it a practice to keep on the lookout for novel and interesting ideas that others have used successfully. Your idea has to be original only in its adaptation to the problem you are working on.
Thomas Edison

Supporting Learning: If pairs of students have difficulty generating many ideas, have them join with another pair to form a small group. Remind students to think of each object's form and potential (curved, pronged piece of metal) rather than its name/usual function of the object (fork, used for eating).

In science the primary duty of ideas is to be useful and interesting even more than to be true.
Arthur Pardee

of the similarities of the things being compared). They can share their answers with other pairs or with the class.

Language Arts Connection: Discuss the use of symbolism in literature. Choose familiar similes or metaphors and discuss their usefulness. Ask: *At what point do these analogies break down? What is the limit of the similarities between the things being compared?*

5.10 Great Examples: Biomimicry

Synopsis: Students research inventions based in nature.

Biomimicry is the use of nature as a source of ideas for inventions. For example, surgical staples were patterned after a practice by some Aboriginal groups of using biting ants to fasten the sides of wounds together. Other examples of inventions based in nature include the following:

Invention/Discovery	Source in Nature	Inventor
1. Velcro	cockleburs	George de Mestral
2. electricity	lightning	Benjamin Franklin
3. telephone	inner ear	Alexander Graham Bell

Have students research an invention that had its source in a natural phenomenon. Add their information to a class chart.

When we try to pick out anything by itself we find it hitched to everything else in the universe.
John Muir

Supporting Learning: Students could begin their research by scanning books and websites on inventions and inventors. Encourage students to share the locations of good sites that they find.

Name: _____

This Reminds Me

What do each the following drawings remind you of? Record three ideas for each drawing.

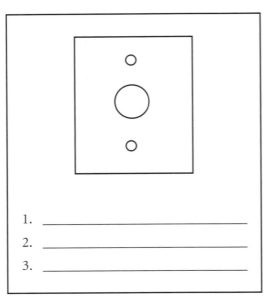

1. _____
2. _____
3. _____

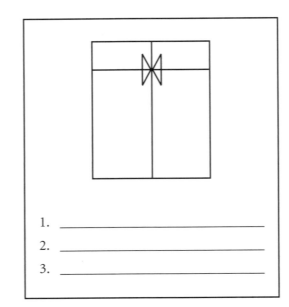

1. _____
2. _____
3. _____

Make two simple drawings and exchange with a friend.

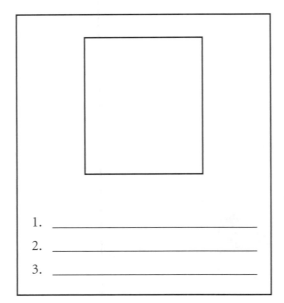

1. _____
2. _____
3. _____

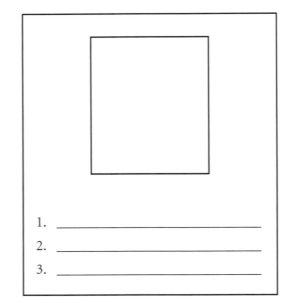

1. _____
2. _____
3. _____

It's Like This!

An analogy is a way to compare two things that are mostly different, but have some qualities in common. For example, a brain is like a book because it is full of ideas. With a partner, cut out all the words below into cards and turn them upside down. Then, turn over any two cards. Using an analogy, explain how one thing is like the other *("A …is like a … because…")*. Place the cards upside down and repeat. You might like to keep track of your favorite analogies to share with the class.

spider web	universe	computer	book	toaster
garden	Internet	apple	bowl	landslide
lighthouse	river	hotel	highway	Sun
brain	ocean	fountain	train	camera
mind	tree	ice cream	cupboard	clock

Worksheet 5B

83

Name: _____

Make a Koch Curve

Simple operations can generate complex patterns. Consider the structure of the Koch Curve (named for the Swedish mathematician who invented it, Helge von Koch). It is said that the Koch Curve has a finite area, but an infinitely long perimeter. You won't be able to draw the whole perimeter, but you can draw enough of it to see that the pattern in a fractal is the same regardless of scale.

1. Draw an equilateral triangle about 9 cm per side. Divide each side of the triangle into three equal segments.
2. Draw an equilateral triangle on the outside of the central segment on each side of the triangle. Divide each external side of the new triangles into three equal segments.
3. Continue to divide and draw as long as you can. Do you notice that the structure of the smallest part is identical to the structure of the entire fractal?
4. Use these same steps with a square. What happens?

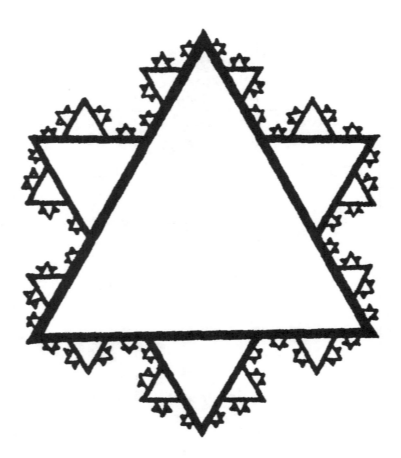

Worksheet 5C

Name: _____

Self-Assessment: Making Analogies

Use the middle column to write your answers to each of the following questions. At a later date, re-assess your skill in making analogies by completing the right hand column.

	Date:	Date:
1. What does "analogy" mean?		
2. What do you think is the purpose of analogies?		
3. Finish this sentence: My life is like … because…		
4. How can you improve your ability to make analogies?		
5. How can you improve your ability to use analogies?		
6. What is one analogy that you find useful in your life?		

CHAPTER 6

Recognizing Patterns

Working with Patterns

6.01 Warm-up; 6.02 Identifying Patterns; 6.03 Recognizing Nothingness; 6.04 Patterns in Data; 6.05 Great Examples: Medical Diagnosis

Playing with Patterns

6.06 Warm-up; 6.07 Moiré Patterns; 6.08 Playful Patterns; 6.09 Great Examples: 1+1=3 or more

Reproducibles

Worksheet 6A: **Sequences**; Worksheet 6B: **Patterns in Data**; Worksheet 6C: **Make a Sierpinski Carpet**; Overhead Projection 6D: **Moirés**; Worksheet 6E: Fowl Patterns; Worksheet 6F: —**READ**—; Self-Assessment: **Recognizing Patterns**

Recognizing patterns is the process of identifying the interrelationship of parts in a whole. It involves finding an arrangement of qualities, form, style, shapes, colors, design, etc. Students can improve their ability to identify and work with patterns by focusing on central features and understanding connections within a system. Pattern skills are important scientific and artistic tools and are used extensively in medicine, engineering, dance, music, art, math, and languages. The related skill of **making patterns** helps students to see how parts fit together to form coherent wholes.

Working with Patterns

6.01 Warm-up

Synopsis: Students brainstorm patterns and identify sequences.

To perceive a pattern means that we have already formed an idea what's next.
Horace Judson

Ask students to name the next letters in this sequence (or choose a sequence appropriate for the level of students):

ABBACABCABBACABC

(The next letters are ABBAC – the pattern is ABBAC followed by ABC)

A sequence is a type of pattern. Ask students: *What other patterns do you know? How do you use your ability to recognize patterns?* Discuss their answers. (The ability to recognize patterns helps to make predictions, formulate opinions, make generalizations, recognize a friend's face in a crowd, hear a

Supporting Learning: Struggling students may benefit from being paired with more confident students to complete Worksheet 6A.

piece of music for the first time and know which group is playing, and understand how things are organized.)

Have students complete and discuss Worksheet 6A: **Sequences**, in which they look for patterns in letters and words. Then students can make sequence puzzles (letters, numbers, objects, etc.) for each other to figure out. [**Answers to Worksheet 6A:** 1.a) size b) alphabetical order c) number of letters 2. Each word has three letters in alphabetical sequence. 4. Students should be able to find at least 20 words: plan, plant, plants, a, an, ant, ants, star, stare, tar, are, rest, strange, stranger, ran, range, ranger, anger, row, wheat, heat, heater, eat, eater, ate, era, rap]

See also: 3.03 What Might Happen?

Math Connection: You might wish to distribute a number grid (e.g., numbers from 1-100) and have students color various sequences or multiples on the grid to create a pattern. They can share and compare their results when they are finished.

6.02 Identifying Patterns

Synopsis: Students find patterns in the classroom.

There are things around us and right at our very feet that we have never seen, because we have never really looked.
Alexander Graham Bell

Ask students: *What do you know about patterns? What patterns can you see as you look around the classroom?* (patterns in wood paneling, wallpaper, book covers, window frost) You may wish to have students check print and online dictionaries for definitions of different types of patterns. Then have students work with partners and search the classroom to make a list of all the patterns they find. Ask: *What could these patterns be used for? Where might other patterns be found?*

See also: 9.06 The Whole Is Greater than the Sum of the Parts

Supporting Learning: Encourage students over the next week to find patterns in various school subjects (patterns in data, events, speech, music, behavior, and in models, stencils, and so on) to reinforce their pattern recognition.

Extension: Have students place a bar magnet under glass or acetate film and sprinkle iron filings or bits of steel wool on the glass (**Caution**: Don't get the filings or wool in the eyes.) Ask students: *What pattern is formed?* (a map of the magnetic field) Have students experiment with two bar magnets with like poles facing and then with unlike poles facing. Move the magnets closer and further apart to observe change in the patterns. Ask: *What do the patterns remind you of? How might you use these patterns in an art project?*

Art Connection: Students may be interested to learn that surrealist artist, Max Ernst, often incorporated random patterns found in wooden floors into his paintings. Ernst would make a tracing (rubbing) by placing paper on the wood and rubbing it with graphite to embellish a painting. Other surrealist painters were inspired by this technique and would trace or copy natural patterns and add them to their art. Students can find and make tracings of various objects in the room or outdoors and incorporate them into works of art.

Technology Connection: Students could choose a pattern found in nature and devise a technique of using it (such as rubbing, tracing, scanning into a computer, using a mirror image on a video camera, or multiple imaging on a still camera). They can experiment with their technique, and then share their method and results with a partner.

Not only science but art also shows us that reality, at first incomprehensible, gradually reveals itself, by the mutual relations that are inherent in things.
Piet Mondrian

Language Arts Connection: Read students a repetitive poem, and have them write their own version using a similar format (such as "Combinations" or "A House Is a House for Me" by Mary Ann Hoberman).

Science Connection: Show students the periodic table of elements and ask them: *What kinds of patterns do you notice in this table?* (color-coded according to metal, metalloid, or non-metal, organized according to atomic numbers, grouped by the number of electron shells) Depending on your students' familiarity with the periodic table, you may want to explain that it is patterned on the chemical properties of the elements. For example, the elements are arranged into periods (horizontal rows) and groups (vertical columns) according to their atomic numbers. In period 1, the elements have a single electron shell, in period 2, elements have two electron shells, and so on. Also, elements that share common chemical properties tend to appear in the same vertical column (group). Ask students to work with a partner to devise another way of organizing the elements using a pattern (e.g., grouping the elements by gases and liquids; metals, non-metals, metalloids; in the order each element was discovered).

See also: *Graphic Representation of the Periodic System During One Hundred Years* by Edward G. Mazurs

Math Connection: Discuss the following quotation with students:

The profound study of nature is the most fertile source of mathematical discoveries.—*Joseph Fourier*

Ask: *What examples can you name of discoveries in mathematics that have come from the study of nature?* (Fibonacci series) *How are these discoveries being used today?* Students can research to find the answers. Ask students to find and display pictures from magazines or newspapers that show the Fibonacci series.

6.03 Recognizing Nothingness

Synopsis: Students examine the role of 'nothing.'

Ask students: *What's the opposite of activity?* (rest) *of 'something'?* (nothing) *What's an example of 'nothing'?* (silence) Play a recording of the opening bars of Beethoven's Fifth Symphony and discuss the role of a pause or rest in music. Ask students to identify the role of 'nothing' in science (the perfect vacuum and absolute zero), and art (negative space, the gaps between objects). You might wish to share the following incident from "The Adventure of Silver Blaze," a Sherlock Holmes mystery by Sir Arthur Conan Doyle. Sherlock Holmes remarks to Inspector Gregory about "the curious incident of the dog in the nighttime." Inspector Gregory protests, "The dog did nothing in the nighttime." Sherlock Holmes responds, "That was the curious incident." Ask: *How might a dog that did nothing be a clue? What other examples can you name of nothing/silence/rest in patterns?*

Have students create puzzles for each other by arranging a collection of objects for a partner to look at briefly. Then students can remove one object from the grouping and ask their partners to look again to detect which object has been removed. Alternately, display the pieces of a relatively simple puzzle (except for one piece) and have students determine which piece is missing

The artist's whole business is to make something out of nothing.
Paul Valéry

Supporting Learning: Struggling students could practise putting sentences or words together without spaces between the words, and then separating the words.

without putting the puzzle together. Students can assemble the puzzle and see if they are correct.

See also: 1.04 Seeing Spaces; 6.09 Great Examples: 1+1=3 or more

Art Connection: Display and discuss examples of Chinese and Japanese script. Point out that the characters are written in imaginary squares which allows for an orderly relationship between the character and the space that surrounds it. Students can practise making characters or letters in lightly drawn squares and then try drawing them in imaginary squares.

Math Connection: Students could create mathematical "What is missing?" questions for each other to solve (word problems with almost—but not quite—enough information to be solved). For example: If each juice bottle costs $1.25, how much will it cost you to buy enough for your party? (missing: how many bottles you need to buy)

Science Connection: In the mid-1800s approximately 60 elements had been discovered. Dmitri Mendeleev, a Russian chemist, created cards for each element, which he then arranged into groups on a wall, looking for patterns among the elements. Mendeleev noticed a pattern when he arranged the elements according to atomic mass, and that pattern became known as the periodic table. However, Mendeleev left gaps (spaces) in his table. Ask: *Why did Mendeleev leave spaces in his table? How did Mendeleev know that there were more elements yet to be discovered?*

Language Arts Connection: Ask students to brainstorm the various forms of poetry patterns (sonnets, couplets, limericks, haiku). Read some rhythmic poems together. Ask: *What is the pattern in each?* (rhyme scheme, number of words or syllables) Have students consider the role of pauses in the meter of a poem. Students might be interested to note that the "lub-dub" rhythm of the iambic pentameter echoes the pattern of the heartbeat and the in/out breath. Students can select sentences from newspapers or magazines to turn into "found poems." They can pattern the words into a certain type of poem (such as a haiku), making small adjustments as necessary to fit the form. They can use the same "found" words to form several types of poems.

6.04 Patterns in Data

Synopsis: Students consider patterns in data.

To see what is general in what is particular, and what is permanent in what is transitory, is the aim of scientific thought.
Alfred North Whitehead

Discuss: *Making sense of the data is a critical part of research. Recognizing patterns is part of organizing facts and understanding what they mean and why they might be important.* Present students with the following real-life example of searching for patterns in data. Scientists wanted to discover how homing pigeons were able to find their way home across great distances. A group of scientists in Italy hypothesized that the sense of smell might be involved in the process. They blocked the birds' sense of smell and discovered that this confused the birds. However, another group of scientists were working on the same problem in Germany. They found that their pigeons were not bothered by losing their sense of smell. Ask students: *What conclusions could you draw by this contradictory evidence?* (assuming that all sources of experimental error were accounted for). *What sort of pattern might you find in the data?* (different pigeons in different places adapt in different ways) Sometimes there is no single answer to a question and that is why the best scientists do not look for *the* answer but for all possible answers.

Challenge: Distribute and discuss Worksheet 6B: **Patterns in Data**, in which students consider the role of paradigms, artifacts, and anomalies in science. You might wish to discuss examples as a class or have students work with partners to answer the questions. Paradigms, artifacts, and anomalies can also be used to understand the patterns found outside of the science lab as well as within it. Ask students to identify examples from daily life.

See also: 3.05 Past, Present, and Future Searches; 8.08 Relationships Among Data

Science Connection: Discuss the patterns that Alfred Wegener considered in developing his theory of continental drift. (the outline of the continents' coasts, particularly, South America and Africa; similar fossil and rock patterns on continents now far apart; geological evidence of climate)

Social Studies Connection: This might be an appropriate time to discuss the collection, analyses, and uses of statistics, especially those concerned with demographics. Discuss the importance of wording questions when gathering statistics and what problems could be caused by "leading" questions. You may wish to have students create or find examples of leading questions, and then discuss how the questions could be improved.

See also: 7.02 How Do You Word It?

Technology/Math/Science/Language Arts Connection: Ask students: *When have you used secret codes or electronic passwords? What kinds of considerations do you need to think about when creating a code or password?* Introduce the terms **cryptography** (secret writing), **cryptanalysis** (the solving of cryptographic systems), and **cryptology** (the science of cryptography and cryptanalysis). Cryptology is based on elementary theorems in number theory. Students might be interested to research the meaning of the root **crypt** (a hidden underground chamber). Ask: *Why is cryptology an important science?* (much of the data in the world is held in computer systems) *What kinds of uses can you name for cryptography?* (protection of confidential company information, telephone calls, credit card orders placed on the Internet; prevent forgery of money, lottery tickets) *What kinds of uses can you name for cryptanalysis?* (breaking codes used for espionage or during war time, e.g., the breaking of the Enigma code) Encourage students to research any of the points mentioned above and to report their findings to the class. You may wish to structure some time for students to work with creating and "breaking" codes.

Career Connection: Have students work together to brainstorm occupations in which pattern recognition is an essential skill (e.g., engineering, dance, music, art, math, and languages). Then they can explain why pattern recognition is important to the occupation and how it is used.

See also: 6.05 Great Examples: Medical Diagnosis.

The most important thing is not any one particular piece, but finding enough pieces and enough connections between them to recognize the whole picture.
Christiane Nüsslein-Volhard

6.05 Great Examples: Medical Diagnosis

Synopsis: Students consider how pattern recognition is used in medical diagnosis.

Many discoveries in medicine arise from pattern recognition: paying attention to new kinds of information or finding new ways to use existent information. An early example of pattern recognition in medical diagnosis and epidemiology was Dr. John Snow's mapping of cholera victims in London in 1854. (He discovered they drank from a common well.) Have students research Dr. Snow's discovery to answer the following questions: *What pattern did Dr. Snow discover among cholera victims in London? How did Dr. Snow discover this pattern? What life-saving application did Dr. Snow recommend?*

Ask students to research or suggest how pattern recognition is used today in medical diagnosis (observations from all the senses and technical information is combined and compared with existing descriptions of disease).

Science Connection: Discuss the mapping of the human genome and the importance of recognizing and analyzing patterns in its research.

Playing with Patterns

6.06 Warm-up

Synopsis: Students represent the pattern of a fractal (a Sierpinski Carpet).

Have students use the instructions in Worksheet 6C: **Make a Sierpinski Carpet** to create a fractal (an irregular shape in which a part is similar in shape to a larger part and a smaller part if it is magnified or reduced to the same size). You may wish to read the instructions aloud so students will not know what the pattern will look like until they are finished. Alternately, if they haven't done so earlier, part or all of the class could use Worksheet 5C: **Make a Koch Curve**. Discuss the patterns formed. Ask: *When have you seen similar patterns? How could you use these patterns?*

See also: 8.04 Making Models; 9.05 Warm-up

6.07 Moiré Patterns

Synopsis: Students learn about moiré patterns.

Ask students: *What do you know about moiré patterns?* (many students may not have heard the name, though they will be familiar with the patterns once explained and shown) A moiré pattern occurs when two or more geometrically regular patterns (lines, circles, dots, and so on) are superimposed and create a new pattern. The pattern is the visual representation of the interference of periodic functions (when two waves are slightly shifted and superimposed, the image formed in the eye is of a new wave with peaks somewhere between the two).

Have students look at the moiré pattern formed when they look through two identical combs held a few centimeters apart or through two layers of window screening. Move one of the combs or the window screen to see changes in the patterns. Alternately, they can look at the moiré pattern formed by a wire screen and its shadow: Look through the wire screen mounted to the window frame with a piece of white cardboard held behind and a bright light shone directly on the screen. Ask students: *What other examples of moiré patterns can you name?* (overlapping picket or chain link fences, sheer nylon curtains, some wallpaper and curtains, intersecting water waves; students may have also viewed moiré patterns formed in printing and scanning when the colored dots do not line up properly)

Supporting Learning: Ask struggling students to name the symptoms of a common cold. Explain that symptoms may form a pattern that the medical practioner can use to help diagnose the sickness.

The mathematician does not study pure mathematics because it is useful; he studies it because he delights in it because it is beautiful.
Henri Poincaré

Supporting Learning: To assess students' understanding of the fractal form, ask them to explain what is meant by an "infinite perimeter but no area."

It turns out that an eerie type of chaos can lurk just behind a façade of order — yet, deep inside the chaos lurks an eerier type of order.
Douglas Hofstadter

Students can create their own moirés by drawing any regular grid of lines (circular, wavy, or straight), then photocopying the grid on clear acetate and laying the acetate over the original gird (or use Overhead Projection 6D: **Moirés** in the same way). Alternately, they can place regularly patterned material such as filters and screens on top of other regularly patterned material to create collages. As students work to complete their moirés, ask them to consider what angles create a moiré. (less than 30°)

See also: Osher and Mishigama's paper, "Moiré Patterns" in Scientific American, May, 1963; 9.06 The Whole Is Greater than the Sum of the Parts

Challenge: Have students create moiré mobiles in which one part of the mobile moving past another part creates a moiré.

Music Connection: Play a two-part fugue, and have students pick out different "voices." Students can listen for one voice the first time through, then listen for the second voice the second time through. You may wish to have them listen a third time to appreciate the "wholes" (harmony) created by the parts (voices). The cassette tape, "Mr. Bach Comes to Call," from the Classical Kids series provides step-by-step instructions on how to make a fugue.

Technology Connection: Students can research technological and scientific applications of moirés. (use of optical grids to detect stress lines in metals and crystals or irregularities in surfaces of fabric or brickwork; use of moiré patterns to measure the topography of 3D objects, and to improve interferometry for X-rays, telescopes, and holograms) They can share their research with the class using an overhead projection or PowerPoint presentation to illustrate their findings.

Math/Music Connection: Natural moiré patterns are created by electromagnetic, acoustical, and water waves. The visual pattern can be used to solve their intersections through a mathematical process called Fourier analysis. Have students research this process and discover its connection to music through its use in electronic synthesizers.

Art Connection: Ask students to research the use of moirés in the artwork of Victor Vasarely. Students may wish to experiment to create similar effects. Have students present their work and discuss how they used moirés.

6.08 Playful Patterns

Synopsis: Students identify patterns in redundancies, oxymorons, and tongue twisters.

Write the following phrases on the board and ask students to determine what pattern they have in common: *free gift, young puppy,* and *big huge.* Students may be able to detect that these are redundancies, patterns in which information given by one feature is repeated in other features. Ask: *What other examples of redundant expressions can you name? How would editing redundancies improve you writing (and speaking)?*

Students can identify the pattern in oxymorons, two words with opposing meanings linked together. (such as exact estimate, act naturally, found missing, definite maybe, genuine imitation, small crowd, "Now, then ...") Ask: *What other examples of oxymorons can you name?* Record their responses. Then ask students to identify the pattern in tongue twisters. (repetition of the initial blend or similar pronunciation) Ask: *What examples of tongue twisters do you*

Supporting Learning: Ask students to look for examples of moirés over the next few days and report back to class on what they find.

I never did a day's work in my life; it was all fun.
Thomas Edison

know? (lemon liniment, truly rural, aluminum linoleum, plain plum bun, Miss Matthew's myth, sixty sticky thumbs). You may wish to have students create their own examples of redundancies, oxymorons, and tongue twisters to share with a partner.

Students could work with a partner to complete Worksheets 6E: **Fowl Patterns** and in small groups to complete 6F: —**READ**— (READ Between the Lines). (**Answers to Worksheet 6F:** 1. man overboard 2. I understand 3. don't over do it 4. just in case 5. backfire 6. bottoms up 7. space invaders 8. time after time [or double time] 9. hitting below the belt 10. just between you and me 11. split second 12. tricycle 13. knee on light [neon light] 14. three degrees below zero **Challenge word:** once in a while)

Technology Connection: Redundancies can be found in many fonts and styles of printed letters. In letters, a redundant feature is one that repeats information given by another feature. For example, a printed upper case A is recognizable without its crossbar. The printed B could be recognized without its vertical line. Students can design an upper case printed alphabet without any redundancies. They can compare their results and discuss how the following quotation applies to their designs:

> The essence of abstracting consists in singling out one feature, which, in contrast to other properties, is considered to be particularly important.—*Werner Heisenberg*

Ask students: *Which feature is particularly important in each letter?* Have students consider various fonts and determine which are the most efficient in terms of their visual appearance. They can share their choices and explain their reasons.

See also: 2.12 Abstractions

Language Arts Connection: Students can create a book using humorous patterns of English modeled on any of the Amelia Bedelia titles by Peggy Parish. The books could be shared with classmates or presented to a younger grade.

Music Connection: Ask students to suggest musical rounds they know (e.g., Row, Row, Row, Your Boat) and sing them together. Discuss and then experiment: *Are the rounds more effective with more or fewer parts?* Alternately, play a drumming rhythm on your desk, and ask students to imitate the pattern. Then students can take turns creating a drumming pattern. Eventually, have one section of the class continue one pattern, while another section plays another rhythm.

Movement Connections: Have students choreograph their own version of a STOMP-type performance (if possible play a video for inspiration) or another type of dance that uses acoustical patterns (e.g., tap dance).

Math Connection: Students can create kaleidocycles, a recent geometric discovery. Kaleidocycles are tessellations on the surfaces of three-dimensional objects. Have students design or use a two-dimensional tessellation pattern and then consider how they can adapt to a simple three-dimensional object, such as a cube. They can research examples of kaleidocycles to share with the class

Art Connection: Students can use a weaving technique and paper or other materials to explore the interconnectedness of two themes, such as art and nature; the individual and society; the microcosm and the macrocosm; or the mind and the universe. For example, in a simple plain paper weave, the weft or woof (strips running side to side) could represent art and the warp (strips

Supporting Learning: ESL students might find it particularly challenging to solve the puzzles in Worksheets 6E and 6F and would benefit from being paired with more confident language users.

We adore chaos because we love to produce order.
M.C. Escher

running up and down) could represent nature. Each strip of paper could have an aspect of its subject written or illustrated on it. Each subject could be a different color.

6.09 Great Examples: 1+1=3 or more

Synopsis: Students consider "in between" figures produced in visual displays.

We used to think that if we knew one, we knew two, because one and one are two. We are finding out that we must learn a great deal more about 'and.'
Sir Arthur Eddington

A famous bit of pattern theory that students might enjoy is Josef Albers' demonstration, "One Plus One Equals Three or More." (In Josef Albers, *Search Versus Re-Search*)
Write this equation on the board:

$$1+1=\ \rule{2cm}{0.4pt}$$

Ask students: *What is the answer?* (2) *You are about to discover that the answer is 3 or more. How can this be?*

This activity works best if a plain background paper, such as white, is used with two strips in another color. Have students cut two vertical strips the same size, several centimeters wide and 6-8 centimeters long. Have them place the strips side by side, with one strip's width between them. Ask: *How many vertical strips do you have?* (They will likely answer 2…1+1=2) But point out that the negative width is also a width and so there are really 3 widths (1+1=3). Discuss: *One line plus one line results in many meanings. Even by making two black lines on paper, a white line seems to appear between them.*

Now have students make an X with their strips. Ask: *How many lines do you have?* (2) *Arms?* (4) Students can imagine where outer lines could be placed to form 4 rectangles, 4 triangles, and 4 squares extending from the middle of the X in between the arms. Have students shift the centers and angles and ask: *What happens to the in-between figures?* (They become unequal.)

Supporting Learning: Struggling students could work with simple two-color patterns, identifying one color as the main component and the other color as the shape formed by the main color.

Discuss: *How might the concept of 1+1=3 be useful in making patterns? How might the existence of the "in-between" figures interfere with the effectiveness of a visual pattern?* (A designer needs to be aware of all the figures that are being created or implied and consider whether each adds to or takes away from the desired effect.) Ask students to find examples of visual patterns which illustrate the concept of 1+1=3.

See also: 1.04 Seeing Spaces; 6.03 Recognizing Nothingness; 6.07 Moiré Patterns; 9.06 The Whole Is More than the Sum of the Parts

Sequences

A sequence is a series of items placed in a certain order. When you see a sequence, ask yourself why it is ordered this way instead of another way.

1. Each of the following sequences has a different reason for its order. What is the pattern behind each sequence?

   Pattern

   a) ant, cricket, python, horse, elephant   _____

   b) ant, cricket, elephant, horse, python   _____

   c) ant, horse, python, cricket, elephant   _____

2. What do these words have in common? (Try to solve the pattern first, but if you are stuck, there is a clue at the bottom of the page.)

   definite   burst   calmness   student   canopy   hijack   coughing

   _____

3. Which words can you find in this circle of letters? Start at any letter and travel in a clockwise direction.

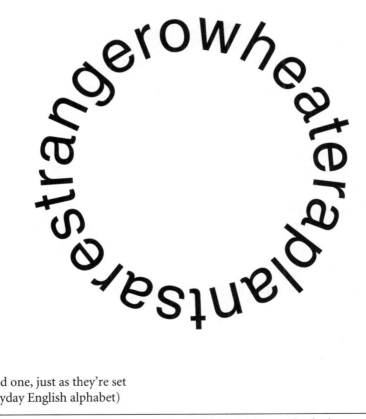

(Clue: 2. Two behind one, just as they're set
          In the everyday English alphabet)

Worksheet 6A

Name: _____

Patterns in Data

A. What is the pattern?

The true worth of a researcher lies in pursuing what he did not seek in his experiment as well as what he sought.—Claude Bernard

Recognizing a pattern is a major step in understanding data. A useful tool for understanding data is a paradigm. **Paradigms** are widely accepted patterns used to set, recognize, and solve problems within a particular field (for example, the concept of latitude and longitude). Paradigms have limits to their use; for example, latitude and longitude do not apply when studying something outside of Earth.

1. Give an example of a paradigm that you have used: _____

2. How did it help you to set up and solve the problem? _____
   _____

3. What were its limitations? _____
   _____

B. Is there something that is not part of the pattern?

Never neglect any appearance or any happening which seems to be out of the ordinary: more often than not it is a false alarm, but it may be an important truth.—Sir Alexander Fleming

Once a pattern has been recognized, it is important to consider (and not discard!) data that do not fit the pattern. **Artifacts** are data that are inappropriate to testing a given theory. These findings may appear to mean one thing but actually mean something else. Artifacts may result from not properly controlling the variables or from not understanding the limits of the theory being tested.

1. Give an example of an artifact from an investigation you have done: _____

2. How did you recognize that it was an artifact? _____
   _____

3. How did you account for it in reporting your results? _____
   _____

C. Is there something that contradicts the theory?

Anomalies are data that contradict a theory even though they are collected while controlling variables in an investigation within the limits of the given theory. Anomalies indicate that the theory may be an inaccurate or incomplete description.

1. Give an example of an anomaly from an investigation you have done: _____

2. How did you recognize it was an anomaly? _____
   _____

3. How did you account for it in reporting your results? _____
   _____

Name: _____

Make a Sierpinski Carpet

A Sierpinski Carpet is a fractal with the interesting properties of infinite perimeter but no area. You won't be able to reach infinity in your drawing, but see how many divisions you can make!

1. Draw a square with 9 cm sides. Divide it into 9 equal squares.
2. Take out (erase or shade in) the middle square.
3. Divide each of the remaining 8 squares into 9 equal squares and take out the middle square of each.
4. Continue dividing and taking out squares as long as you can. Do you notice that the total perimeter of all holes continues to increase as the remaining area decreases? Imagine how this would look in 3D.
5. Try the same operations with an equilateral triangle.

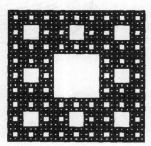

Moirés

Name: _____

Fowl Patterns

A. Why did the chicken cross the road? Maybe some of these animals know the answer. Follow the pattern, then add three "cross the road" jokes of your own.

Why did the turtle cross the road? *To get to the shell station.*
Why did the turkey cross the road? *It was the chicken's day off.*
Why did the otter cross the road? *To get to the otter side.*
Why did the chicken cross the road by the playground? *To get to the other slide.*

Create three more "cross the road" jokes:

1. _____
   _____

2. _____
   _____

3. _____
   _____

B. Suppose some of the world's best minds were put to work to solve the "Why did the chicken cross the road?" question. Perhaps some of their answers might look like this:

Albert Einstein: *Whether the chicken crossed the road or the road moved beneath the chicken depends upon your frame of reference.*
Charles Darwin: *Chickens, over great periods of time, have been naturally selected in such a way that they are now genetically disposed to crossing roads.*
Sir Isaac Newton: *Chickens at rest tend to stay at rest. Chickens in motion tend to cross the road.*

Now add three more answers from the point of view of other famous people. Exchange with a partner and see if they can guess who might have said each.

1. _____
   _____

2. _____
   _____

3. _____
   _____

Worksheet 6E

Name _____

— READ —

What is the name of this worksheet? (read between the lines)

Put your creativity to work solving the following expressions. The first two are done for you.

COVERSREADCOVERS
(read between the covers)

WEAR
LONG
(long underwear)

1. MAN
   BOARD

2. STAND
   I

3. DON'T
   DO IT

4. *CAJUSTSE*

5. *ERIF*

6. *S*
   M
   O
   T
   T
   O
   B

7. *VAD ERS*

8. *TIMETIME*

9. *THE*
   BELT
   HITTING

10. *YOUJUSTME*

11. *SEC   OND*

12. *CYCLECYCLECYCLE*

13. *KNEE*
    LIGHT

14. ZERO
    B.A.
    M.A.
    PH.D.

Challenge Word: WOHNICLEE

Worksheet 6F

Name: _____

Self-Assessment: Recognizing Patterns

Use the middle column to write your answers to each of the following questions. At a later date, re-assess your skill in recognizing and forming patterns by completing the right hand column.

Finish these sentences	Date:	Date:
1. One way I would like to use a pattern is…		
2. The amazing thing about patterns is…		
3. My favorite pattern is…because…		
4. I can recognize patterns when …		
5. Recognizing patterns helps me…		
6. Making patterns helps me…		

CHAPTER 7

Solving Problems

Defining the Problem

7.01 Warm-up; 7.02 How Do You Word It?; 7.03 How Else Can You Think About It?; 7.04 The Bare Bones; 7.05 Great Examples: Great Problem Solvers

Problem-Solving Techniques

7.06 Warm-up; 7.07 Thinking it Through; 7.08 Breaking Assumptions; 7.09 Sources of Inventions; 7.10 Great Examples: Making the Invisible Visible

Reproducibles

Strategy Spot 7A: **Prepare for Problem Solving**; Strategy Spot 7B: **Prepare for Decision Making**; Worksheet 7C: **The Bare Bones**; Strategy Spot 7D: **Working Through a Problem**; Worksheet 7E: **Colorful Countries**; Strategy Spot 7F: **SCAMPER**; Self-Assessment: **Solving Problems**

Solving a problem includes working through a process to identify possible solutions and selecting the best one. Defining a problem is a large part of solving a problem, whether it is a scientific investigation or a day-to-day decision. Students can strengthen their ability to approach a problem in an organized way by working with a variety of problem-solving techniques and applying them to different situations. Problem-solving skills are called upon in every walk of life, especially in the legal professions, counseling, police work, city planning, engineering, architecture, medicine, and business. The related skill of **making decisions** helps students to understand the needs of the various parts of a situation and choose appropriate action from a range of possibilities.

Defining the Problem

7.01 Warm-up

Synopsis: Students consider what all problems have in common.

Ask students: *What do you know about the game of Tic-Tac-Toe? How is it played? What do you think is the best strategy for winning?* Have students play a game of reverse tic-tac-toe. (To win, a player tries to force the opponent to make three X's or O's in a row). After students have played several rounds, ask: *What strategies did you use when playing reverse tic-tac-toe? How did you discover these strategies?*

Problem-finding is just as important as problem-solving but much more difficult and much more rare.
Edward De Bono

Ask students to think about a time when they solved a problem. This could be a mathematical problem, a relationship problem, a scheduling problem, or any other kind of problem. Ask students to reflect on this problem for a few minutes and then record in their notebooks what the problem was, the steps they took to solve it, and the effectiveness of the solution. They can record their answer to this question: *How might you solve it differently now, if the same problem came up again?* Ask for volunteers to share their reflections. After discussing several, ask: *What do all problems have in common? What are the stages in solving a problem?* (Classically, the stages are identified as preparation, incubation, inspiration, and verification. Students may have other perspectives, such as defining the problem, considering all points of view, considering possible solutions, and choosing the best solution) Ask: *What advice do you have about the best ways to solve problems?*

Supporting Learning: Encourage students to consider problem solving like playing a game, cracking a code, or solving a mystery.

Have students record a current problem they would like to solve, and answer these questions: *What different approaches could I use for this problem? What could I learn or do that would make it easier to solve?* Students can try out their approaches and record their progress in their journal over the next few days. Invite students to share their results with the class.

7.02 How Do You Word It?

Synopsis: Students choose the best way to word questions.

It isn't that they can't see the solution. It is that they can't see the problem.
G. K. Chesterton

Ask students: *What do you know about Lewis Carroll?* Students may be familiar with the works of author Lewis Carroll (real name: Charles Dodgson), but may not know that he also gained fame as a mathematician and logician. Write these questions posed by Dodgson on the board and ask students to answer them in their notebooks:

1. Which is better: a clock that is right once in two years or a clock that is right twice a day? Why?
2. Which is better: a clock that loses a minute a day or one that doesn't run? Why?

Supporting Learning: Ask students to picture clocks with faces, not digital clocks.

Students might think that the obvious answers are 1. A clock that is right twice a day, and 2. A clock that loses a minute per day. After students have given their answers (and if no one has noticed that both questions are about the same two clocks) ask students to compare the clocks in the two questions. Ask: *How many clocks are being described?* (the same two clocks in both questions) A clock that loses a minute each day is right once in two years, and a clock that does not run at all is right twice a day. Whether one clock sounds better than the other depends on how the problem is stated. Then ask: *Why is it important to carefully consider the way you word a question? What other examples can you name in which the wording of a question or problem produces different results?*

Have students consider and discuss the following problem: *Imagine there is a very busy intersection near the school that is difficult for students to cross safely. Frame the problem as a question. For example, you might choose one of the following: How can the road be made safer? How can drivers improve their skills? How can students be more careful when crossing the road?* Have students work in small groups to think about the various questions they might ask. Then have all groups present their choice of question and the reasons for it. Discuss how each question might influence the type of answer that is found.

Extension: Ask students: *What does forming a question help you to do?* (know what you are looking for) *Why is it important to know what you are looking for?* (you can recognize it when you see it) *How can you know what you are looking for when you are investigating something new?* (you can't) *Why is the phrasing of the question especially important when you don't know what you are looking for?* (you remain open to a wide variety of possibilities and do not pre-determine a narrow range of possible answers)

See also: 3.02 What Would You Like to Know?; Strategy Spot 3A: **What Are the Questions?**; 6.04 Patterns in Data, Science Connection

Science Connection: Ask students to revisit questions that they have considered in investigations in science class. Ask: *How else could these questions be phrased? How might the rewording affect the methods, outcomes, or conclusions of the investigations?*

Discuss the following quotation by physicist Richard P. Feynman:

> The problem of creating something which is new, but which is consistent with everything which has been seen before, is one of extreme difficulty.

Ask: *Do you think it is easy or difficult for scientists to decide which questions to investigate? Why?*

Career Connection: Ask students to name some occupations that interest them. Record half a dozen suggestions on the board, and then consider the first one. Ask: *What problems need to be solved in this occupation?* Brainstorm a variety of answers. Then have students work alone or with a partner to brainstorm problems that need to be solved in the other occupations. These problems could include both daily tasks and long-range goals for the occupation as a whole. Invite students to share their answers.

7.03 How Else Can You Think About It?

Synopsis: Students prepare to solve problems.

Discuss the following quotation:

> You can never solve a problem on the level on which it was created.—*Albert Einstein*

Ask: *What do you think Einstein meant in this quotation? What experiences have you had that are examples of this quotation?* Students can discuss how it helps to step out of the problem and view it from a different perspective, or re-assess a problem after getting some rest or gathering more information about it.

Ask: *What steps can you take to prepare you to solve a problem?* Record responses on the board (or have students record in their notebooks). Distribute and discuss the points from Strategy Spot 7A: **Prepare for Problem Solving**, in which students consider step-by-step instructions to analyze a problem. Have students make additions to their recorded list, as needed. Ask students to discuss and list the steps involved in making decisions. Then have them compare their list with Strategy Spot 7B: **Prepare for Decision Making**.

See also: 3.03 **What Might Happen?**

Supporting Learning: Reinforce the point that the more problem-solving techniques a students can use, the more choices there are in how to reach a solution, and the more adaptable they can be in solving problems.

Extension: Students can try other ways of thinking about and representing a problem. Encourage students to use an existing cartoon and replace the caption with their own words to describe the problem, or draw a cartoon that represents something about the problem. They could also think of a song, television program, or movie title that captures the essence of the problem.

Art Connection: Discuss examples students may know (from their own experience or lives of artists) in which an artistic breakthrough resulted from solving a problem that was thought to be unsolvable. For example, a large block of marble was in storage for forty years in Florence because several sculptors had tried to sculpt it but had failed and declared it wasn't useable. Michelangelo took the marble from storage and carved it into "David." Ask: *What are some problems you have faced in creating an art project that initially you did not think you could solve? How did you go about finding a solution?*

7.04 The Bare Bones

Synopsis: Students learn a technique for organizing information.

Ask students: *How does organizing information help to solve a problem?* Ask students to work in small groups to list and sketch examples of all the types of graphic organizers they know (e.g., concept map, flow chart, timeline, events chain, Venn diagram, storyboard, tree diagram). Students might not be familiar with a technique for organizing themes and ideas for problem solving called a "herringbone" (also known as fishbone, skeleton). A herringbone chart is useful for displaying cause and effect patterns, and for considering all the different parts of a situation to determine where more data or information is needed. You may wish to distribute Worksheet 7C: **The Bare Bones**, and summarize one way of using a herringbone chart as follows:

The most successful people in life are generally those who have the best information.
Benjamin Disraeli

- ✓ Write the problem in the "head" of the chart.
- ✓ Write each major cause of the problem along a rib on the left hand side. For each major cause, ask, "Why does this happen?" List the minor causes around the rib.
- ✓ When all causes are identified and grouped around the appropriate ribs, brainstorm solutions for each cause.
- ✓ Record the solutions on the right hand side of the ribs.

Ask students: *What did you find helpful about using a herringbone chart? What was challenging? What else could you use a herringbone chart for?*

See also: 7.10 Great Examples: Making the Invisible Visible; 8.07 Representing and Communicating Data

Language Arts Connection: A herringbone chart can be a source of ideas to be developed into poems. Students could use each of the "bones" as the basis of a stanza or verse, or combine several of the bones to create a figure a speech.

Social Studies Connection: Discuss the margin quotation by Disraeli. Explain that Benjamin Disraeli was the Prime Minister of Britain in the late 1800s. Ask: *What might Disraeli have meant by the "best" information? Why would it be important for a country's leader to have the best information?* You may wish to discuss examples students have studied in which the quality of information determined the success or failure of a political (or other)

Supporting Learning: You may want to have all students use the chart to analyze the same problem. Then they can share and compare their charts and incorporate ideas from other charts.

undertaking. Ask: *How does the quotation apply to a community leader? To an environmental concern? To a recent news event? To students?*

7.05 Great Examples: Great Problem Solvers

Synopsis: Students consider factors that affect problem solving and productivity.

We haven't got the money, so we've got to think.
Sir Ernest Rutherford

Ask: *What circumstances might contribute to how much a person is able to accomplish or how many problems they are able to solve? How closely is problem solving tied to having the means (money, equipment, time) available? What factors determine how many problems you solve in your life?* You may wish to refer to the margin quotation by Rutherford.

Discuss the connections between problem solving and productivity. Some influential scientists, artists, and inventors have had long careers with high productivity. For example, Thomas Edison established a quota for himself to create a minor invention every 10 days and a major invention every 6 months. By the end of his life Edison held 1,093 patents (including patents for the microphone, the record player, and the first practical electric light bulb). Albert Einstein produced 248 publications in 53 years; Sigmund Freud produced 330 publications in a 45-year career; and Pablo Picasso created several thousand works in his 75-year career as an artist.

Other influential scientists, artists, and inventors produced relatively few breakthroughs. For example, Hans Selye, the Canadian researcher who pioneered the concept of physiological stress, commented that despite having an extensive staff and the most up-to-date equipment in later years, he regretted not being able to "add anything comparable in its significance to those first primitive experiments."

Supporting Learning: Encourage students to view problems as challenges that they can work through. Have students provide explanations in their portfolios to describe why they selected each piece.

Encourage students to create portfolios of their best work in each subject and from outside of school. Have students discuss how and why they selected each piece. Ask: *What problems did you have to solve to complete this work? Why is it important to keep examples of your best work?*

Music Connection: Students can choose from several famous composers and research the circumstances of their lives that may have added to or detracted from their potential to produce music. Ask: *What examples can you find of composers who overcame great problems to create?* (e.g., Beethoven – deafness; Mozart – lack of funding) Students can share their research Ask: *What qualities do the composers have in common?*

Problem-Solving Techniques

7.06 Warm-up

Synopsis: Students notice their problem-solving techniques.

We are usually convinced more easily by reasons we have found ourselves than by those which have occurred to others.
Blaise Pascal

Ask students: *What are some ways of solving problems you have used in math and other school subjects?* Some problems are solved by being broken into parts, and dissected with questions. Other problems are solved by experiment and "guess and check." Still others can be solved through reflection, creative thinking, and intuition. In the process of solving a problem one might visualize, rearrange words, or use mathematical symbols, or make a model. Record students' answers on the board.

Students can notice their own problem-solving techniques in the following activity. Ask students to try to draw a circle (freehand) as accurately as possible moving their pencil in a clockwise direction. Give them several minutes to practice drawing circles. Then ask them to draw circles counterclockwise. After a few minutes ask them to change the speed of drawing, sometimes drawing circles very quickly, and sometimes very slowly. Have students try drawing circles holding the paper in a different way and then holding the pencil in a different way.

Discuss experiences. Ask: *What was easier, what was harder, and why? What did you notice about your problem solving in each instance? What can you infer about problem-solving processes based on your experience?* Students may comment that initially they had to get used to a new perspective or use new skills, and that with practice each drawing became easier.

See also: 7.07 Thinking it Through, Math Connection

Supporting Learning: Some students may have difficulty drawing realistic circles. Encourage them that the point of this activity is to become more aware of how they use techniques, rather than how well they can draw.

7.07 Thinking it Through

Synopsis: Students use problem-solving skills and strategies to play a game.

Ask students: *What games have you played that use problem-solving skills? What was challenging about the games?* Have students play games such as chess, hangman, charades, Battleship, or Dictionary (see directions below). Then have them analyze the strategies and problem-solving skills they used in playing the games. You might distribute Strategy Spot 7D: **Working Through a Problem**, which provides suggestions for working through a problem. (See also 4.09: Are Two Doctors a Paradox?) Ask students: *Which strategies did you use from Strategy Spot 7D in playing your game? How might you incorporate the strategies that you did not use?*

The process of research is to pull the problem apart into its different elements, a great many of which you already know about. When you get it pulled apart, you can work on the things you don't know about.
Charles F. Kettering

To Play Dictionary:
- A moderator selects a word at random from the dictionary which none of the players is familiar with. Each player writes a definition for the word (on the same type and size of paper) based on what they think it could mean, and phrased to sound like a real dictionary definition. The moderator writes the actual definition (on the same type and size of paper).
- The papers are collected, mixed, and each definition is read aloud by the moderator. Then each definition is read a second time and the players record their vote for the definition they think is the real one.
- Points are given to players who choose the correct definition, and also for each vote they received for their own definition. This game will challenge creative, deductive, and inferring skills.

Supporting Learning: Help students realize that problem solving is not limited to school subjects, but is a skill that they will use many times in their lives. Like other skills, it can be improved and made easier and more effective with practice.

Language Arts Connection: Students can design and create posters for the classroom featuring proverbs or quotations about working through problems (e.g., "Problems worthy of attack show their worth by hitting back," "If at first you don't succeed, try, try, again," "Well begun is half done"). Students could create their own quotations, rhyming couplets, or slogans, or they can research what others have said, such as

> A problem well stated is half solved.
> *John Dewey*

> To raise new questions, new possibilities, to regard old problems from a new angle requires creative imagination and marks real advances in science.
> *Albert Einstein*

> If I had eight hours to chop down a tree, I'd spend six sharpening my axe.
> *Abraham Lincoln*

Math/Social Studies Connection: Discuss the following question: *What is the fewest number of colors you would need to color a map so that no two regions sharing a boundary line had the same color?* Students can examine some maps and/or draw maps to experiment with. They could also import and color maps using the computer. According to the Four-Color Theorem, four colors are sufficient for any map. Students can research the theorem (and its variations). Then challenge them to color in Worksheet 7E: **Colorful Countries** using only three colors.
See also: 2.12 Abstractions
Math Connection: Review with students the problem-solving methods that they know for solving mathematical problems (e.g., GRASP: Given, Required, Analysis, Solution, Paraphrase). Ask: *Which methods have you used successfully? Which methods have you not yet tried?*
See also: 7.06 Warm-up

7.08 Breaking Assumptions

Synopsis: Students break assumptions to solve a puzzle in different ways.

Ask students: *What "mind puzzles" have you tried to solve?* Discuss examples.

Draw a grid of nine dots (3 x 3) on the board. Ask students to copy the grid onto their paper and devise a way to connect the nine points using *five* straight lines without lifting their pencil from the paper. Give students 5 minutes to complete the activity, and then share the answers.

Then ask students to draw a new grid of nine dots and connect them using *four* straight lines without lifting their pencil from the paper. Some students may already know an answer from having solved this problem before; other students may declare this 'unsolvable'. Discuss the answer(s) that students have found, and determine what assumptions they had to break in order to find the solutions. (They may have broken the assumption that the lines cannot extend beyond the imaginary square formed by the dots and drawn a triangle connecting 7 dots and a straight line through the center connecting the remaining two.)

Ask students to determine how many other ways the problem could be solved and identify which assumption they had to break in each instance. (Or give them each of the following assumptions and have them work from there.) Invite students to share solutions.

For a long time I considered even the craziest ideas about the atomic nucleus…and suddenly I discovered the truth.
Maria Göppert-Mayer

✓ *How could you connect all the dots by using only three lines?*
If you break the assumption that the line must pass through the center of the dots, three zigzag lines can angle through the dots.

✓ *How could you connect all the dots by using one line?*
If you break the assumption that the line must be thin, one thick line can cover and connect all the dots.

If you break the assumption that you may not crease the paper, it can be folded so that one line connects them all.

If you break the assumption that the paper must be flat, one spiral line can encircle the cylinder. Likewise, one spiral line could encircle the Earth twice and pass through the dots.

If you break the assumption that you cannot rip the paper, the dots can be torn out and piled up and one line can go through them all.

Extension: Have students reconsider a problem they are trying to solve using Strategy Spot 7F: **SCAMPER**, which includes suggestions for considering a problem in different ways.

See also: 1.10 Warm-up; 1.11 How Do You Look at It?; 2.01 Warm-up; 2.05 Have You Seen My Elephant?; 3.08 Discovering; Strategy Spot 3B: **Keep an Open Mind**

Supporting Learning: Encourage struggling students by discussing that sometimes difficulty in a subject is not because they *cannot* understand it, but only because they have not yet found a method that makes sense to them. Remind them to be open to new ways of learning about a subject.

Math Connection: Ask students: *If one hundred artists were asked to paint the same flower, would all the hundred paintings be the same? If one hundred mathematicians were asked to solve a problem, would all one hundred methods be the same?* Students may find the answer to the first question obvious but may not be sure about the second question, since many times they have been taught only one way to solve a type of problem. The answer to the second question is also no. For example, there are more than three hundred ways to prove the Pythagorean theorem. Ask students to add 36 and 67 in their heads, and then have them describe how they did it. Some may add 36 and 67 in columns; some may have added thirty plus sixty, and then added six plus seven to the result; or some may have rounded up or down. List all the possible ways students can think of to solve the equation. Ask: *Why might it be useful to know many ways of solving a mathematical problem?*

7.09 Sources of Invention

Synopsis: Students problem solve to improve the design of objects.

Ask students: *What ideas have you had for improving the design of something? What have you ever wished was designed better?* Ask students to select two objects at random and place them on their desk in front of them. You may wish to have all students use the same two items, such as a pencil and an eraser, or a notebook and a ruler. Have them list the attributes of each item on a sheet of paper. For each attribute have them ask themselves: *How else can this be accomplished? Why does this have to be this way?* Then have students record their ideas for how the objects might be changed to become more effective. Discuss their suggestions.

Some men see things as they are and ask why. Others see things that never were and ask why not.
George Bernard Shaw

Extension: Have students consider the question: *Does real creativity come from using the things we create or from creating the things we use?* Ask students to explain their answers. One way to invent something is to think of what is needed. Another way to invent something is to consider the materials and think about what uses they suggest. Ask students to debate the pros and cons of each approach.

Supporting Learning: Some students may have difficulty in identifying attributes and considering alternate designs. Pair them with a more confident learner, or meet with them in a small group and work through the activity together.

Students can divide into small groups to work with various building sets and materials. Some groups can start from an idea of the finished product and select the pieces they need to create it. Other groups can examine the building materials they have been given, think about the uses the materials suggest, and work from there. After the projects are finished students can compare their processes and results.

See also: 2.11 The Shape of Things to Come; Worksheet 2G: **The Shape of Things to Come;** 5.08 What Might Be

Technology Connection: Discuss the motto of the 1933 World's Fair in Chicago:

Science Finds, Industry Applies, Man Conforms

Students can discuss why it may have been chosen, and whether they feel the message (and language) is relevant or appropriate today. Encourage students to use the same format to create a motto for the relationship among science, technology/industry, and humans that expresses their own point of view. Remind them to use inclusive language. A motto suggested by Donald A. Norman in *Things that Make Us Smart* is: People Propose, Science Studies, Technology Conforms.

7.10 Great Examples: Making the Invisible Visible

Synopsis: Students consider the role of visual representations in solving problems.

Probably it's better to put off using words as long as possible and get one's meaning as one can through pictures or sensations.
George Orwell

Ask students: *When you think about a problem, do you "see" the problem or do you think in words about it? When have you used visual representations (pictures, mind maps, charts, etc.) to solve problems?* Some problem solvers find it helpful to see the problem. Leonardo da Vinci and Galileo Galilei are two examples of creative people who used drawings, diagrams, and graphs as a way of formulating and solving problems. Richard P. Feynman collected and rearranged information into what is now called Feynman diagrams and made it possible to visualize a world that was previously unimaginable. Albert Einstein said that he thought visually, and did not believe that words and numbers played a significant role in his thought processes.

Discuss with students: *Do you find it easier to learn information by seeing it in a chart, reading it, or by hearing it described? Which formats do you prefer to use for sharing information?* You may wish to distribute **Checklist: 150 Ways to Use Information** found on page 12.

Supporting Learning: You may wish to make notes about each student's preferences for style of learning and sharing information.

Ask students: *What role can technology play in problem solving?* They can discuss the benefits of computer simulation and modeling in solving problems with components that are too large, too small, or too difficult to represent in other ways.

See also: 7.04 The Bare Bones; 8.07 Representing and Communicating Data

Strategy Spot

Prepare for Problem Solving

Solving problems is a process that can't be predicted. You can help the process by keeping an open mind and by considering many questions and well as many answers. Use these strategies to help you identify the problem.

1. **Start by figuring out exactly what needs to be determined.** The tricky part is not solving the problem, but figuring out what the problem is. Restate the problem at least three times to generate different perspectives. Write the problem you want to solve as a question. Remember, there is not only one way to define a problem. Your initial question should be fairly broad and should open up possibilities. For example, if the school cafeteria is too crowded at lunch, you might ask,

   How can school lunch be made less crowded?

   Try to avoid "solution-minded" questions that close the possibilities, such as

   How can we get a bigger room? or How can students eat in shifts?

2. **Brainstorm ideas about the problem.** Use a diagram, a mind map, or concept map to help you brainstorm. At this stage you cannot determine what the steps are to solving the problem. Accept that you do not yet know what to do or what to think. This stage is about getting down some thoughts about the problem and exploring possible directions. Record observations, questions, and ideas.

3. **Ask yourself what the problem is like.** If it were a circus, how would you visualize your problem? How is your problem like a garden? A machine? Record your answers.

4. **Imagine you are the problem.** For example, if you were the school cafeteria, how would you organize yourself to provide more room? How does it feel when you are too crowded?

5. **Review your ideas from Steps 2, 3, and 4.** Group ideas into themes. For example, your comments about the arrangement of chairs and tables could be grouped as a theme. Another theme might be about the scheduling of the lunch break. Another theme might be about using other locations.

6. **State each of your themes as a fairly broad question.** Create a concept map or mind map for each theme, including possibilities of how the question might be answered. Explore the advantages and disadvantages of each possibility. Consider the opposite of each question. For example, if you ask, "How can we arrange the chairs so the entrance area is more open?" ask yourself, "How can we arrange the chairs so the entrance area is more blocked?" Sometimes a clue to the answer lies with its opposite.

Worksheet 7A

Prepare for Decision Making

A good way to make a decision is to talk it over with someone. Putting your thoughts into words will help you clarify how you feel about it. The following steps may be helpful when you are not sure which decision to make.

1. **Try to understand the situation.**
   Exactly what needs to be decided? Get as much information about it as you can. Restate it in your own words.

2. **Check your feelings.**
   What initial reaction do you have to the situation? What does the "best" part of you think about the situation?

3. **Consider the needs of each of the people involved (including you!)**
   Who will be affected by the outcome of the decision? How might the decision affect each person?

4. **Play with the information.**
   Make a sketch of it. Compare this decision to other decisions you have made. Look at it from different points of view.

5. **Consider all the decisions that could be made in this situation.** Write down all the different decisions, even the ones you do not think you would choose. For each decision, write down what might happen if you chose it.

6. **Determine the best and worst cases for the situation.**
   What do you need to do to achieve the best outcome? What do you need to do to avoid the worst outcome?

7. **Sleep on it.**
   It is easier to find solutions when you are well rested.

8. **Choose the best decision and consequences.**
   Be able to explain why you chose this outcome rather than the other choices.

9. **Take action.**

Worksheet 7B

Name: _____

The Bare Bones

Use a herringbone chart when you want to display cause and effect patterns, or to help you determine where more data or information is needed. Write the problem in the "head" of the chart. Then write each major cause of the problem along a rib on the left hand side. For each major cause, ask, "Why does this happen?" List the minor causes around the rib. When all causes are identified and grouped around the appropriate ribs, brainstorm solutions for each cause. Record the solutions on the right hand side of the ribs.

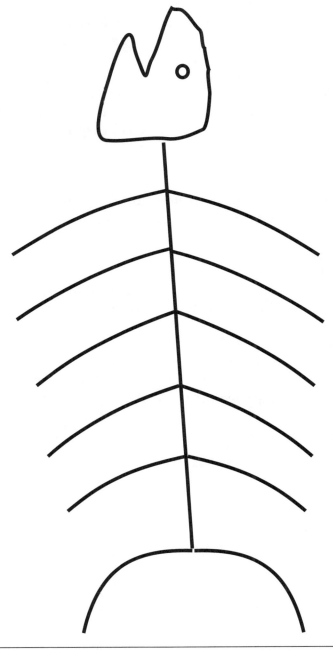

Strategy Spot

Working Through a Problem

If you get stuck as you work through a problem, try one (or more) of these strategies.

1. **Change the problem.**
   Make your problem more abstract and less specific. Restructuring can help you to think more broadly and be less attached to preconceived notions of what the solution should be. For example, if you work with "transportation to school" you will have more possibilities than if you work with "getting my Mom to drive me to school." Restructure whenever there is too much information to keep track of or when interesting and surprising aspects of the problem emerge.

2. **Take a different point of view.**
   Identify with part of the problem (even if the part is an object or a process) and try to see the problem from that perspective. Ask yourself, "How would I feel if I were… What recommendation would I make?" You can also take the perspective of a professional or expert. Ask yourself, "How would an expert in this field approach this problem?"

3. **Create a paradox.**
   Change some of the words that describe the problem to their opposites. Ask yourself, "What is the opposite or contradiction of the problem?" Summarize your paradox in two words and then draw what the two words remind you of.

4. **Look beyond the first answer.**
   Make a habit of searching past the first answer that seems like it will work. Sometimes there is something a little better if you dig a little deeper. Don't expect to be right the first time.

5. **Pre-solve the problem.**
   Imagine that the problem is already solved in the best possible way. Write down how it was solved, and which people or events made it possible. Work your way back to the current situation. What else do you need to do or know to help move the problem closer to its solution?

Worksheet 7D

Name: _____

Colorful Countries

You can use only three colors to color this map. The same color cannot share a borderline with itself. Take a few minutes to plan how you will solve this puzzle before you begin to color.

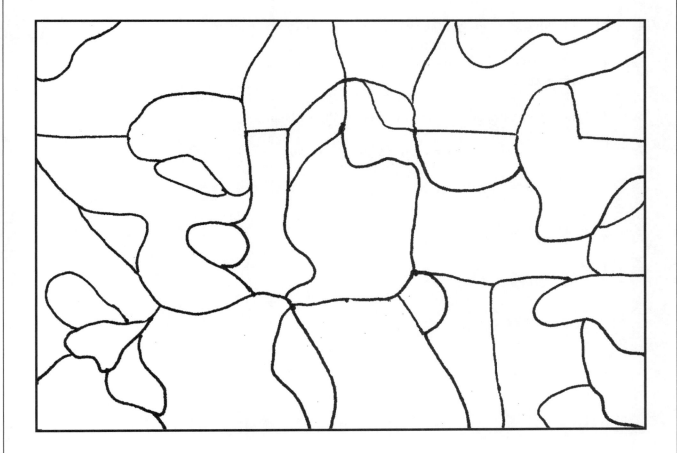

SCAMPER

Why not SCAMPER your way through a problem or decision? Try these steps.

1. **S**   Substitute one word for another in your problem. Simplify.

2. **C**   Combine, connect, communicate.

3. **A**   Adapt something from another field or another problem to help you. Approach someone for his or her input. Accept that some problems take more time to solve.

4. **M**   Modify and magnify. Make it smaller, bigger, clearer, or easier.

5. **P**   Put the big problem into smaller chunks and solve those first. Have patience.

6. **E**   Eliminate extra details. Find the essence. Enjoy the process.

7. **R**   Rearrange, reverse, restructure, rethink, and relax.

Name: _____

Self-Assessment: Solving Problems

Use the middle column to write your answers to each of the following questions. At a later date, re-assess your skill in solving problems by completing the right hand column.

	Date:	Date:
1. a) What is one of the best decisions you ever made? b) What was good about it? c) How did you arrive at that decision?		
2. Finish this sentence: I make my best decisions when…		
3. a) What was one of the most difficult problems you have ever solved? b) What made it difficult?		
4 Finish these sentences: a) When I'm faced with a decision I… b) When I'm faced with a problem I…		
5. What is your plan for improving your ability to make decisions?		
6. What is your plan for improving your ability to solve problems?		

Transforming

Transforming is the process learners go through when internalizing new information by linking it to their own language, experience, and knowledge and then presenting the knowledge in a different way. The transforming process incorporates two or more thinking tools serially (such as observing and abstracting, or naming, visualizing, and connecting). Students can use transforming skills to think dimensionally (visualize geometric shapes), to make knowledge relevant, to create models, and to communicate their knowledge to others through a variety of formats. Transforming is especially useful in teaching, engineering, designing, architecture, computing science, medicine, visual arts, and mathematics. The related skill of **making models** helps students to create a mental image or physical representation to explain an object, event, or process.

Changing the Form of Information

8.01 Warm-up

Synopsis: Students transform understanding into communication.

Ask students to describe a toy "transformer" — or better yet, bring in one or more if you have one (or ask students to bring some in). After students have had a chance to manipulate or discuss the toys, ask: *What do you think "transform" means?* (change from one thing into another). *When have you used transforming skills?* Discuss the point that the value in understanding something is not just to possess the information, but also to use it or apply it in some way (transform it).

I learned long ago that being Lewis Carroll was infinitely more exciting than being Alice.
Joyce Carol Oates

One way of activating or consolidating an understanding is to communicate, or share it. Ask students to think of something interesting they have learned recently and then complete the following sentence stems about it.

1. *The amazing thing about this is …*
2. *With this information I can …*
3. *Now I understand that …*
4. *This information will help me to …*

Ask students to share their sentences with a partner.

If students have not already done so, they can use **Checklist: 150 Ways to Use Information** on page 12 to keep track of the various ways in which they use information, and to inspire them to try new ways.

Extension: Students could design simple transformer toys out of building sets or other materials.

Language Arts Connection: Have students consider Joyce Carol Oates' quotation from the margin. Ask: *What do you think Oates' quotation means? Do you agree or disagree with the quote? Why? What experiences of your own does this quotation remind you of? What does the quotation have to do with the process of transforming?*

Supporting Learning: Check in with students several times over the next few weeks to see how they are doing with using the Checklist.

8.02 Transforming Raw Material

Synopsis: Students draw cartoons about the process of transforming raw material into a finished product.

A rock pile ceases to be a rock pile the moment a single man contemplates it, bearing within him the image of a cathedral.
Antoine de Saint-Exupéry

Share with students the quotation in the margin by Saint-Exupéry. Ask: *How does the quotation connect with experiences you have had? What other examples does this quotation remind you of?* Discuss the processes that would change a rock pile into a cathedral. Students could work with a partner to draw a labeled diagram, events chain, or cartoon-type illustration of the quotation or show the transformation of a rock pile into a cathedral, an idea into a published book, a concept into a film or website, or an industrial process.

Extension: Students can use Worksheet 8A: **Transform Your Knowledge** to practise transforming the understanding they have gained in class into a variety of expressions.

See also: 5.03 It's Like This!

Math Connection: Ask students to identify how transformational thinking is applied in mathematics. (A problem is presented in a numerical form, and a person might convert it into a picture, mentally manipulate the picture, and then transform it into an equation, words, or model.) Ask students what is meant by the following expression: "Every equation has its physical manifestation and every physical phenomenon its mathematical model."

Supporting Learning: Less confident learners might choose a process that is outlined in a science or other textbook. They could first explain the process to you, and then represent its steps.

Art Connection: Discuss the following quotation by Pablo Picasso:

Some painters transform the Sun into a yellow spot; others transform a yellow spot into the Sun.

Ask: *How would you describe this quotation in your own words? How does this quotation apply to an experience you have had?*

Drama/Movement/Art/Music/Language Arts Connection: Students can also paint, draw, dance, or act out what they hear in music. They could play a game of charades, choosing song, film, or book titles to act out.

Language Arts Connection: Have students practise their transforming skills by making concrete poetry (using words to create images). Alternately, they could suggest their favorite rebuses (such as those on personalized license plates) and design and illustrate them for a partner to solve.

8.03 Working Within Limits

Synopsis: Students consider the role of limits in structuring transformation.

Survey students: *How many of you tend to do homework as soon as you can after it is assigned? Why? How many of you tend to put it off until the last possible moment? Why?* Share the following quotation by musician Duke Ellington:

I don't need time. What I need is a deadline.

Ask: *What do you think this quotation means? What experiences from your life does this remind you of?* Then write the following quotation by architect Frank Lloyd Wright on the board:

Limits are an artist's best friend.

Ask students: *Do you agree with Wright's quotation? Why or why not? What experiences have you had on which to base your opinion? What might be meant by "limits" in art? In science? Would limits be a scientist's best friend? Why or why not?* Students may note that limits can help us to think beyond an obvious solution and find answers or expressions we might not otherwise have discovered. Have students consider how they might incorporate their feelings about limits into their scheduling of their homework.

Extension: Students can debate the above questions, either formally or informally.

Music Connection: Students can try singing words to familiar songs to different tunes. For example, many songs can be sung to the tune of "Greensleeves" or "Twinkle, Twinkle, Little Star." (The song "Amazing Grace" can be sung to the tune of "The House of the Rising Sun," and "The Lion Sleeps Tonight" as well as to "Greensleeves")

See also: 8.09 Great Examples: Sound Transformers; 9.02 Linking Physical Sensations

Science/ Movement Connection: Have students consider how it feels to be a molecule confined by the limits of state by having students line up in molecule formations: solids packed tightly together, liquids less tightly packed but within the limits of the "container" and gases moving about freely.

Science Connection: Discuss the importance of placing limits on an investigation by controlling variables. Ask students to explain variables (the conditions or factors that can influence the outcome of an investigation), controlled variables (the conditions that are not allowed to change), manipulated variables (the conditions that are changed in order to see the effect of the change), and responding variables (the conditions or outcome that is changed as a result of changing the manipulated variables). Ask: *What is the benefit of having only one or two manipulated variables in an investigation?*

If you ask me to write a song about the ocean, I'm stumped. But if you tell me to write a ballad about a woman in a red dress falling off her stool at three in the morning, I'm inspired.
Stephen Sondheim

Supporting Learning: If a formal debate is structured, build into the marking process each team's ability to listen to, and carefully consider others' opinions.

Math Connection: Ask students: *What do you know about the game of chess? What move can a knight make?* (A knight can move two squares in one direction and one square in a perpendicular direction. No two chess pieces can occupy one square at the same time, though a knight may pass or jump over occupied squares on its way to an empty square.) Present students with this challenge:

Imagine a chessboard made of just nine squares (3x3). Suppose you were to place a white knight in each of the two corners of the board nearest you, and a black knight on each of the furthest corners. Moving one at a time, and following the rules stated above, how few moves would it take so that the whites and blacks would change places?

Students can draw the board and use markers or colored paper as knights, or they can figure out a way to devise the answer without needing to try the moves. After students have solved the puzzle they can share and explain their method. (**Answer:** 16. Students can find how to calculate the answer at http://mathforum.org and elsewhere on the Internet.)

8.04 Making Models

Synopsis: Students consider the benefits of using models.

The purpose of models is not to fit the data, but to sharpen the questions.
Samuel Karlin

Ask students: *What do these things have in common: clay, origami, sculpture, equations, building sets, and holograms?* (they can all be used to model something) *What is a model?* (a mental image or physical representation that helps to explain an object, event, or process) *When have you made a model or used a model?* (atomic model and particle model from science, building sets, models of cars and airplanes) *What are some of the ways in which models are useful?* (help visualize something that is either too small or too large to be seen directly; help answer questions like, "Will it work?" "How long will it last?" and "How does it need to be modified?"; help plan experiments; communicate findings to other researchers)

Have students take out a sheet of paper, and ask them: *What can this paper be used to model?* Prompt students' thinking by having them complete the following sentence stem: "A blank piece of paper is like…" Students may suggest a variety of responses, including geometric shapes, origami, airplanes, and so on. Have students create a model using the piece of paper (and as few other materials as possible) to share with the class.

Students can complete Quotes and Notes 8B: **Model Quotations** in which they relate a quotation about the use of models to their own experience.

Supporting Learning: Collect and assess students' responses to Quotes and Notes 8B: **Model Quotations**. Watch for an understanding of the concept of a model and students' ability to relate the quotation to their own life.

Extension: Have students share their interpretation of the following quotation by philosopher Arthur Koestler. (Depending on your students' prior knowledge, you may first need to explain that Sir Isaac Newton's observation of a falling apple helped lead to his discoveries in the field of gravity and that Paul Cézanne was a painter famous for his still life paintings of apples and other objects.)

Newton's apple and Cézanne's apple are discoveries more closely related than they seem.—*Arthur Koestler*

Ask: *What does this quotation say about the connections between science and art? How does this quotation relate to the use of models?*

Social Studies Connection: Ask students to list the various ways models are used in Social Studies and to find examples of each.

Art Connection: Discuss the use of models in art (objects for still-life, people for figure drawing, smaller 3-dimensional models for larger sculptures or installations, and so on).

Share the following quotations with students:

> I long ago came to the conclusion that even if I could put down accurately the thing I saw and enjoyed, it would not give the observer the kind of feeling it gave me. I had to create an equivalent for what I felt about what I was looking at.—*Georgia O'Keeffe*

Ask: *How can you explain O'Keeffe's quotation in your own words? According to this quotation, in what way could all art be considered a model?*

Technology Connection: Many manufacturing processes involve bending, folding, and pressing 2-D materials into 3-D shapes (cardboard boxes, pipes and cans from sheet metal). Have students research and report on one of these processes, including the role computer modeling plays in developing the processes.

Math Connection: Ask students to visualize each of the following three-dimensional shapes: sphere, cube, prism, pyramid, and tetrahedron. Encourage students to visualize the inner structure as well as the surface shape, and to try manipulating them mentally from all sides, including inside. As a challenge students can try visualizing more complex shapes, such as an octahedron, icosahedron, or dodecahedron. They may wish to investigate the relatively new field of mathematics called *plication* (the folding of geometric shapes).

See also: 1.06 What Do You See?

Math/Science Connection: "Fractal geometry" models natural objects more closely than do most geometric examples. It is especially useful in modeling clouds, mountains, turbulence, coastlines, blood vessels, and roots and branches of trees. Students can research the use of fractal geometry in modeling.

See also: 8.07 Representing and Communicating Data; Worksheet 5C: **Make a Koch Curve**; 6.06 Warm-up; Worksheet 6C: **Make a Sierpinski Carpet**; 9.05 Warm-up

8.05 Great Examples: Model Inventors

Synopsis: Students match inventors and discoveries with models.

Ask students: *Who do you think is the most famous inventor? What did he/she invent? How is that invention being used today?* Students can work in small groups to list inventors and their inventions. Then they can meet with another small group and play "Name the Invention/ Inventor." Each group can take a turn naming either an invention (or an inventor), and the other group guesses the inventor (or invention).

Have students complete Worksheet 8C: **Model Inventors**, in which students match the inventor to the invention and the model for the invention. Students may have to research some of the answers. Extra spaces are provided for students to add more examples from their prior knowledge. Alternately, before

A scientist needs an artistically creative imagination.
Max Planck

Nothing is more important than to see the sources of invention which are, in my opinion, more interesting than inventions themselves.
 Gottfried Whilhem Leibniz

copying the page, you might wish to add other names, discoveries, and observations that the students have already studied. Discuss the simplicity of many of the observations that led to important discoveries. (**Answers:** 1. George Westinghouse; an efficient way to transmit clean natural gas to homes and industry; simple well in his backyard 2. Stephanie Kwolek; Kevlar® — a polymer fiber five times stronger than steel; pearls on a string 3. Charles Eames; comfortable, visually pleasing chair designs; custom-fitted plywood splints for wounded soldiers 4. Leonardo da Vinci; sound travels in waves; circles form when a pebble is dropped in water 5. Bessie Nesmith; Liquid Paper®; white tempura paint 6. René Descartes; dynamics of the cosmos; clock's mechanics 7. Joseph Paxton; The Crystal Palace — the world's first glass-and-iron building in structure of giant water lily 8. Archimedes; principle of displacement; water overflowing a bathtub 9. Igor Stravinsky; a new musical style; folk music).

Dimensional Thinking

8.06 Warm-up

Synopsis: Students estimate time.

The ability to estimate time, space, weight, distance, and proportion is part of the skill of transforming. Ask students: *How well can you estimate the passage of time? How long is 30 seconds? A minute? Five minutes?* As you time 30 seconds, ask students to close their eyes and put up their hand when they think 30 seconds has passed. Try this again using a different time interval.

Have students brainstorm activities that they think will take 30 seconds to complete (e.g., tying a shoe, walking down the hall to the water fountain). In pairs, have one student perform the activity, while the other times their partner. How long did the activity take to complete?

Ask: *How do you use your ability to estimate time in your daily life?* Discuss students' responses. Ask: *How does the passage of time seem to vary depending on whether you are enjoying an activity or whether you are not?*

Extension: Students could devise activities to check their abilities to estimate space, weight, distance, and proportion.

Career Connection: List the following occupations on the board: biologists, geologists, astronomers, biochemists, nurses, and architects. Ask students to arrange them in order of occupations dealing with the largest distances to occupations dealing with the smallest distances. (**Answer:** astronomers, geologists, architects, nurses, biologists, and biochemists). Ask students: *Which occupations deal with even smaller distances?* (chemists and physicists) Ask: *How might challenges differ between occupations concerned with very tiny distances and those with great distances? Which type of occupation appeals more to you? Why?*

Then have students consider time. Ask: *Which occupation deals with trillionths of a second?* (physicists) *Which deals with thousands of years?* (archaeologists, paleontologists, historians) *Which deals with millions of years?* (astronomers, geologists) Ask: *How might challenges differ between occupations concerned with very brief passages of times and those with long passages of time? Which type of occupation appeals more to you? Why?*

Supporting Learning: As students make their Venn diagrams, they may find it useful to refer to **Checklist: 150 Ways to Use Information** from the Introduction to this book.

8.07 Representing and Communicating Data

Synopsis: Students consider ways of representing and communicating data.

Ask students: *How can data be represented?* (charts, prose, graphs, diagrams, models) *Which formats have you used to communicate data?* Discuss student responses and the merits of each format. Ask: *How do charts or graphs aid in understanding the data?* (the information can be seen all at once) *How does a model aid in understanding the data?* (models deal with a small scale, manageable version instead of the data) *How does a PowerPoint presentation aid in understanding the data?* (it breaks the information into segments or events)

Have students work in small groups to create a 3-way Venn diagram to illustrate various ways to represent and communicate data. One circle could include oral formats (such as speech, song, radio show), the second circle could include visual formats (such as a graph, photo essay, illustration), and the third could include written formats (such as a summary, essay, directions). The overlapping sections could include formats that include oral, visual, and written components (such as a board game, video production, or model). Students may find it is easier to start by brainstorming different types of formats and then sorting them into categories. Have groups present and explain their Venn diagrams.

See also: 7.04 The Bare Bones; 7.10 Great Examples: Making the Invisible Visible

Art/Music/Drama/Movement Connection: Ask: *How could data be expressed through dance? Through painting? Through songs? Through skits?* Students can find and share examples of how information can be expressed through the fine arts. For example, there are a number of songs about science principles, social studies facts, and so on (such as those found at www.songsforteaching.com). Data from patterns such as fractals has been transformed into paintings. Students may be interested to note that researchers in neurology and physics have transformed data into dance and dance notation and found both beautiful results and a new way to understand and appreciate the layers of data. Music and dance data — as well as wind, humidity, and temperature data — have been digitized, transformed into numerical tables, and used as a source for variable values, which have been mapped to create architectural forms. Students can choose some data they are working with in one of their school subjects and find a way to communicate it using the fine arts. They may wish to work with a partner or in small groups.

See also: 8.04 Making Models; 8.09 Great Examples: Sound Transformers; 9.02 Linking Physical Senses

Career Connection: Ask students: *Which occupations require the ability to represent data clearly? Explain your answer.* Then divide students into two teams. Each team can select several occupations that they think do *not* require clear representation and communication of data. They can exchange their list with the other team and then have a five-minute session in which to brainstorm all the ways those occupations *do* require communication of data.

8.08 Relationships Among Data

Synopsis: Students consider positive and negative features in data representation.

Ask students: *What do you know about space junk?* (Space junk includes "dead" satellites, specks of paint, lost tools, and pieces of machinery used to repair space stations that orbit Earth. The space junk moves at tremendous speeds, in different directions, and at different levels through space. When collisions occur, even more debris is created.) Highlight the importance of keeping track of where all the "junk" is since even a small object, such as a speck of paint can have the effect of a bullet hitting a space shuttle or satellite. Ask: *What system could be used to keep inventory of all the space junk?* In groups, have students brainstorm possible tracking methods. Encourage groups to research how space junk is currently tracked and stored.

Ask students: *What questions need to be considered whenever there are data to display?* (How can the relationships among data be arranged clearly and effectively? How can the most data be displayed without becoming too complex and difficult to understand?) Whenever there are data to display, it is best to communicate the information as simply and clearly as the amount and type of data allows. Ask: *What would be an effective way to show what percentage of the class speaks a second language other than English?* (a pie graph) *What would be an effective way to show the distance a car travels in one hour?* (a line graph with "distance" on the x-axis and "time" on the y-axis) *What would be an effective way to show the average monthly temperature in our community?* (bar graph with months on the x-axis and temperature on the y-axis).

Ask: *What are some things a website designer might have to think about when displaying graphs and diagrams?* (how to use empty space, whether to use bright or subdued color, which labels and how many to use, how to encourage the viewer to compare data rather than be diverted by the display itself, how to present many numbers in a small space). With these points in mind, have students search for good examples of visual representations of data in magazines, on websites, or in other sources. They should choose several examples and be able to explain why each is effective. Students could also find examples that do not work well (such as long pages of text that is not broken by headings, or graph paper that is darkly lined so that the graph is difficult to see). Have students present and explain their examples.

Supporting Learning: Have students look through examples of their own work and assess how effectively they have displayed data. Ask: *How could you improve your ability to effectively share data?*

Art Connection: Students can consider the juxtaposition of data; in other words, what happens when information is placed side by side. For example, suppose a photograph of some adventurers in a sports utility vehicle is placed beside a third-world farm family in a bullock cart. Ask students: *What types of questions, associations, or ideas might that arrangement suggest?* (Is one mode of transportation better than the other? Might the adventurers prefer to experience the slow and easy pace of a bullock cart? Which vehicle is more efficient for the purposes it is used for?) Have students choose several evocative images and place them side-by-side. They can share and discuss their arrangements.

See also: 6.04 Patterns in Data; *Envisioning Information* and *The Visual Display of Quantitative Information* by Edward Tuft (These books pre-date computer technology, but are nevertheless useful resources for the principles of visual representations.)

8.09 Great Examples: Sound Transformers

Synopsis: Students investigate the transformation of data into sound.

An interesting field in transformations is that of data into sound. When genetic sequences are transformed into music, researchers can hear similar sequences more easily than when they scan for them visually (the ears can perceive complexity that the eyes cannot – such as being able to pick out the sounds of different instruments while listening to an orchestra as a whole). Musicians are also experimenting with producing music that interprets statistical databases and DNA. Students can meet in small groups and predict some uses for the new technology and speculate about future breakthroughs. They can share their ideas with the class.

See also: 8.04 Making Models: Music Connection; 8.07 Representing and Communicating Data: Art/Music/Drama/Movement Connection

Career Connection: Ask students to consider the possibilities opened up to individuals by the transformation of data into sound (for example, visually impaired individuals can take an active role in research). Ask: *What new occupations might arise? What aspects of this field appeal to you? What would you like to learn more about? How might you find your answers?*

See also: 8.07 Representing and Communicating Data; 9.02 Linking Physical Senses

To my mind, the laws which nature obeys are less suggestive of those which a machine obeys in its motion than those which a musician obeys in writing a fugue, or a poet in composing a sonnet.
Sir James Jeans

Supporting Learning: Encourage students' understanding that new occupations are being created all the time, and that they may have many opportunities in their lives that they cannot even imagine now.

Name: _____

Transform Your Knowledge

How many different ways can you express your knowledge about something? Choose a concept (something that you know) and transform it in each of the following ways. An example of a concept could be a fact "bodies at rest tend to stay at rest" or an observation "the darkest hour is just before dawn."

1. **Explain it.** Explain the concept in your own words.

_____
_____
_____

2. **Give examples of it.** When and where have you seen this concept at work?

_____
_____
_____

3. **Apply it.** Use the concept to explain something you have studied.

_____
_____
_____

4. **Justify it.** How could you test this concept?

_____
_____
_____

5. **Compare and contrast it.** Relate it to other concepts. How is it similar and different?

_____
_____
_____

6. **Put it in the context of the whole.** Where does this concept fit in to the topic that it is part of? Why is it important? What role does it play?

_____
_____
_____
_____

7. **Generalize it.** What general principles are included in this concept?

_____
_____
_____

Worksheet 8A

Quotes and Notes: Name:_____

Model Quotations

Each of the following quotations is about the use of models.

Storytelling reveals meaning without committing the error of defining it.

Hannah Arendt

Art does not reproduce the visible, but makes visible that which is not easily seen.

Kimon Nikolaides

It's simple, you just take something and then you do something to it, and then you do something else to it. Keep doing this and pretty soon you've got something.

— artist Jasper Johns on being asked to describe the creative process

A theory has only the alternative of being right or wrong. A model has the third possibility: it may be right, but irrelevant*.

Manfred Eigen

*irrelevant means it does not apply

If I have any technique at all, it simply consists of my making one new model after another until I happen to hit on the one that seems likely to work best.

C.W. Fuller

1. Choose the quotation you like best. Who is it by? _____

2. Explain it in your own words. _____
_____
_____

3. Give an example of how it applies to an experience you have had. _____
_____
_____

Name: _____

Model Inventors

In the chart is a list of several well-known inventors. Below the chart, in a mixed order, are the inventions and the observation each invention was modeled on. Complete the chart by matching the discovery or invention, and the observation it was modeled on, to the inventor. You may have to research to be sure of all your answers. Then add several more examples that you know or have found through your research and exchange with a partner.

INVENTOR	This discovery/ invention...	Was modeled on this observation...
1. George Westinghouse		
2. Stephanie Kwolek		
3. Charles Eames		
4. Leonardo da Vinci		
5. Bessie Nesmith		
6. René Descartes		
7. Joseph Paxton		
8. Archimedes		
9. Igor Stravinsky		

Discovery/Invention

The Crystal Palace, the world's first glass-and-iron building

principle of displacement

a new musical style

dynamics of the cosmos

an efficient way to transmit clean natural gas to homes and industry

Liquid Paper®

comfortable, visually pleasing chair designs

Kevlar®, a polymer fiber five times stronger than steel

sound travels in waves

Observations

clock's mechanics

simple well in his backyard

white tempura paint

circles form when a pebble is dropped in water

cantilevered rib structure of giant water lily

pearls on a string

water overflowing in a bathtub

custom-fitted plywood splints for wounded soldiers

folk music

Worksheet 8C

Name: _____

Self-Assessment: Transforming

Use the middle column to write your answers to each of the following questions. At a later date, re-assess your skill in transforming by completing the right hand column.

	Date:	Date:
1. Finish this sentence: To me, transforming ideas means…		
2. When have you used your ability to transform ideas?		
3. Finish this sentence: Transforming ideas helps me to…		
4. Finish this sentence: Making models helps me to…		
5. How can you improve your ability to transform ideas?		
6. How can you improve your ability to make models?		

Worksheet 8D

CHAPTER **9** # Synthesizing

> **Body Thinking**
>
> 9.01 Warm-up; 9.02 Linking Physical Senses; 9.03 A Natural Act; 9.04 Great Examples: If I Were an Electron
>
> **The Whole Is Contained in Every Part**
>
> 9.05 Warm-up; 9.06 The Whole Is Greater than the Sum of the Parts; 9.07 Aha! 9.08 Ten Wonderful Things; 9.09: Great Examples: A Personal Hall of Fame
>
> **Reproducibles**
>
> Quotes and Notes 9A: **If I Were an Electron**; Worksheet 9B: **My Personal Best**; Self-Assessment: **Synthesizing**

Synthesizing is the process of putting together parts to form wholes. It involves a simultaneous integration of many higher-order thinking tools, such as observing, visualizing, and empathizing, so that memory, knowledge, imagination, and feelings are understood and appreciated in a holistic way. This ability to unite parts into wholes is especially useful to scientists, athletes, actors, musicians, physicians, and artists. The related skill of **empathizing** helps students to find within themselves a reflection of the outer world.

Body Thinking

9.01 Warm-up

Synopsis: Students describe experiences of "body thinking."

How do I know about the world? By what is within me.
Lao-tse

Supporting Learning: Students sometimes are not aware that they have not understood something in class. Learning to notice and respond to physical sensations can help them increase their awareness of when to check their understanding.

Ask students: *When you are sitting in a class and do not understand what is being taught, how do you feel physically? What symptoms do you notice of physical discomfort? How might you use those signals as indicators of when to ask for help? What do you notice about your physical sensations when you know an answer and have your hand up to answer? How else can you "think" with your body?* Discuss examples from sports, dance, drama, playing a musical instrument, using tools or operating machinery, puppetry, and so on.

The following activity can help students to be more aware of their physical sensations. Ask students to try to walk in a straight line on a level surface with their eyes closed. Their partners can watch them for safety concerns while they walk, and to observe which direction their partner tends to deviate in. With this information, students can again try to walk in a straight line, slightly correcting their direction. Students can switch roles, and continue to practise a few more times and judge whether they are consistently going in the same direction. (This tendency to deviate in one direction slightly is a reason why people who are lost sometimes walk in circles.) Discuss how they sensed which direction they were going in and how they corrected themselves.

See also: 1.05 Using All Your Senses; 1.06 What Do You See?; 9.02 Linking Physical Senses

9.02 Linking Physical Senses

Synopsis: Students experience one sense in terms of another.

Ask students to imagine life as an ant. (If weather and circumstances permit, they might go outside for this activity, or crawl about inside the classroom.) Ask: *How does it feel to peer through blades of grass, and look up at all the bigger creatures? How does it feel to climb up and over mounds of dirt?* Discuss other aspects about the experience that students suggest. Ask students: *What books or films have you read or seen that featured a person changed into an animal or object, shrunken or expanded, or of a different age? How did the characters cope? What did the characters learn from the experience?* Some students may have visited museums, zoos, or science centers that included devices and displays that simulate how a creature sees or hears. Ask students to share their experiences.

Extension: For more experiences in synesthesia (linking of physical sensations) have students reflect, record, and then discuss their answers to these questions:

Supporting Learning: If some students have difficulty in responding to the **Extension** questions, ask them to choose their favorite number and color, and to explain their choices.

What does the number nine feel like?
What does Sunday taste like?
What does the idea of happiness look like?
What shape is yellow?

Have students create similar questions to exchange with a partner. Then, have students discuss their answers.

See also: 5.04 Personal Analogies; PBS television series, "Kratts' Creatures."

Art/Music Connection: Students can make transpositions between musicians and artists that they are familiar with. For example, if Van Gogh were a rock star, who would he be? If Beethoven were a painter, who would he be? Have students give reasons for their choices.

Drama Connection: Have students make a list of inanimate objects, such as a piece of toast, a sidewalk, and a traffic light. Ask students to choose an object to act out and have classmates guess what it is.

Science/Technology Connection: The linking of physical sensations is necessary in both virtual reality and robotics. For example, in the Telepresence Surgery System (TeSS), a virtual-reality machine enables surgeons to operate on people from miles away by electronically manipulating a surgical robot. Atomic-force microscopes can magnify the pull experienced by a microscopic needle in the presence of a layer of atoms. Physicists who use these microscopes can actually "feel" the texture of a single layer of atoms and "sense" the physical attraction of individual ions. Have students investigate TeSS or other recent inventions in robotics and virtual reality.

Language Arts Connection: Students may be familiar with the "Magic School Bus" books and television cartoon series (the books are written by Joanna Cole). If so, discuss students' favorite episodes/volumes. If not, share part of one of the books with the class. Ask: *If you were a "magic school bus" where would you go?* Students could write and illustrate a book (or paragraph) to describe where they would go and what they would hope to learn.

See also: 1.05 Using All Your Senses; 1.06 What Do You See?; 9.01 Warm-up

9.03 A Natural Act

Synopsis: Students practise empathy for objects and events.

After I have identified myself with a tree, I create an object which resembles a tree, the sign of a tree.
Henri Matisse

Supporting Learning:
Empathizing with the concept being studied can help students improve their ability to recall information. You might wish to make a point of encouraging students' empathizing skills over the coming weeks.

Have students form into small groups to play "nature charades" in which they choose and act out simple phenomena such as wind, hail, a volcano, or a waterfall and then progress to more complex natural events, such as a rock slide, the seasons, migration, or the movement of the tides. Ask students to guess which natural phenomenon each group is enacting. Then discuss how acting the role of a natural phenomenon helps to find a piece of nature within oneself that reflects the outer world (empathy). Ask: *How did it feel to be the natural phenomenon you were portraying? What understandings are you able to gain through empathy that are not available through other means?*

Have students use a similar approach when studying or reading, by asking themselves questions like, "What would this carbon atom want to do? How did the volcano feel right before erupting? How does the storm look from the cloud's perspective?" These questions can help students find connections between the natural world and sensations and emotions within themselves.

Invite students to practise mimicking or imitating the sounds and behavior of natural phenomena. Then have students play a second round of "nature charades" in which they can only make sounds (no motions) to represent a natural event or phenomenon.

See also: 1.07 What Do You Recall?; Worksheet 1A: **What Do You Recall?** 1.08 Tips for Memorizing and Recalling; Strategy Spot 1B: **Tips for Recalling**; 2.07 I Am a Part of All I Have Met; 9.04 Great Examples: If I Were an Electron, Career Connection

Music Connection: Discuss the following quotation by violinist Yehudi Menuhin:

> I can only think of music as something inherent in every human being. Music coordinates mind, body, and spirit.

Ask: *What might be the benefits to the musician from playing music? What might be the benefits to the listener? Why might it be important to coordinate mind, body, and spirit?* If any students are musicians, invite them to comment on their experiences of practising and performing.

Drama Connection: Re-enactment is an important tool for understanding a story, process, history, or event. Students can work in small groups to choose an event they are currently studying in one of their school subjects (or in community news) and create and perform a skit re-enacting the event. Alternately, they could choose a story or scene from a film to re-enact. Ask: *What new appreciation of the event/scene do you have as a result of performing it? How might the skill of re-enactment be helpful in your daily life?*

9.04 Great Examples: If I Were an Electron

Some scientists have found it useful to imagine themselves as part of the subjects they are studying. Ask: *How might identifying with the subject help a scientist to answer questions and understand processes?* Have students complete Quotes and Notes 9A: **If I Were an Electron**, in which they match quotations to the scientist who made them. (**Answers:** 1. Barbara McClintock; 2. Joshua Lederburg; 3. Jacques Monod; 4. Ernest Rutherford; 5.Subrahmanyan Chandrasekhar; 6. Richard P. Feynman; 7. Hannes Alfven; **Challenge Answer:** These scientists are all Nobel Laureates.)

See also: 1.09 Great Examples: Great Observers; Worksheet 1D: **How Do Others See It?**

Career Connection: Share with students the following quotation by Charles F. Kettering, director of research of General Motors for many decades. When engineers got too involved with complex calculations and models, he would say something like, *"Yes, but do you know what it feels like to be a piston in an engine?"* Ask: *How might feeling like a piston help the engineers?* Sometimes people who work with machinery, play musical instruments, or are active in sports involving equipment (such as tennis, golf) report that at times they feel the object they use is like an extension of their body. Have students interview someone who manipulates machinery, technology, or equipment of some type, and ask about their ability to "sense" or "feel" what the equipment is doing. How does this sense help them to be successful?

See also: 9.03 A Natural Act

The Whole Is Contained in Every Part

9.05 Warm-up

Ask students: *What is a quest? What fictional heroes do you know who have gone on a quest? What historical figures do you know who have gone on a quest? What movies, television programs, comic books, video games do you know in which the main character is on a quest? How are male and female quests similar? Different?*

Students can work with a partner and choose one of the discussed quests that they are both familiar with. Ask them to identify and discuss the parts of the quest and how they contribute to the quest as a whole. They can choose a way of representing their ideas, such as in a chart, illustration, poster, skit, cause-and-effect diagram, and so on.

Language Arts Connection: Discuss the margin quotation by Chesterton. Ask students: *What do you think this quotation means? Do you agree or disagree? Explain your answer.* Students can write fables and ask a partner to try to identify the moral. Alternately, you can provide students with a moral and have them develop a fable to express it. Then they can share and appreciate the variety of ways the same moral can be shown.

Art Connection: Discuss the following quotation by Peter London:

The first purpose of art is wholeness.

Ask students: *What does this quotation mean to you? In what ways do you agree with this quotation? In what ways would you change this quotation?*

I think the most helpful suggestion that can be made…as to how one may get new ideas in general [is]… 'sympathetic intuition' or 'empathy'… You should enter into your problem in such a way that you almost become part of it.
Sir Karl Popper

Supporting Learning: Encourage students to research each quotation's source by using the scientist's name and learning what she/he is famous for, or by searching for the quotations on the Internet.

Fable is more historical than fact, because fact tells us about one man and fable tells us about a million men.
G.K. Chesterton

Supporting Learning: If students are unsure of how to develop a story from a moral, ask them to describe an experience of their own the moral reminds them of. They can write their experience as a story or in anecdote form.

Science Connection: Discuss the following quotation by Jacob Bronowski:

All science is the search for hidden likeness.

Ask students: *What experiences of your own does this quotation remind you of? How else might you define science?*

Music Connection: Composer Arnold Schonberg once commented, *"Whatever happens in a piece of music is nothing but the endless reshaping of a basic shape."* Ask students to find a piece of music they think exemplifies this quotation, and bring it to class to share.

Math Connection: Fractals are irregular shapes in which any part is similar in shape to a larger part and a smaller part if it is magnified or reduced to the same size. Students can draw fractals using Worksheet 5C: **Make a Koch Curve** and Worksheet 6D: **Make a Sierpinski Carpet**. After they are finished ask, *What do the fractals remind you of? How does a fractal represent the expression "The whole is contained in every part"?*

See also: 5.03 It's like This!: **Math/Art Connection;** 6.06 Warm-up; 8.04 Making Models

9.06 The Whole Is Greater than the Sum of the Parts

Synopsis: Students show that the whole is greater than the sum of the parts.

Science is built with facts as a house is with stones—but a collection of facts is no more a science than a heap of stones is a house.
Henri Poincaré

Ask students: *What is meant by the expression, "The whole is greater than the sum of the parts"? What examples can you name of this expression?* Then discuss the margin quotation by Poincaré. Ask: *What more is science besides a collection of facts?*

The following demonstration allows students to experience the concept of the whole being more than the sum of the parts. (You may wish to practise the demonstration before performing it for the class. The trick is to wrap the string very tightly.) Display a strand of raw spaghetti and ask whether it is strong enough to resist much force. Break it, and then show that even a handful of spaghetti can be broken at once. Then display a piece of string and discuss its qualities. Wrap the string tightly around a handful of spaghetti, encircling it from top to bottom. Challenge any student to break it in half. Ask students: *Can you explain what happened when we combined weak spaghetti strands and weak string?* (a strong whole was produced)

Ask students: *In what other ways can you demonstrate or represent the principle that the whole is more than the sum of the parts?* (e.g., a finished picture from a pile of puzzle pieces, a house from a collection of building blocks) Students can work individually or with a partner to make representations or demonstrations to share with the class.

Supporting Learning: If time and supplies allow, allow students to try the spaghetti/string activity for themselves.

Extension: The spaghetti/string activity was a favorite demonstration of inventor R. Buckminster Fuller. Students could research how Fuller's inventions exemplify the principle of the whole is greater than the sum of the parts (geodesic dome, Dymaxion Air-Ocean Map, Dymaxion car, Dymaxion house, world peace game). If you can find a copy of Fuller's 1970 book, *I Seem to Be a Verb*, (written with Jerome Agel and Quentin Fiore), display and discuss its format with students. Ask: *How does the format of this book show the principle of the whole is greater than the sum of the parts?*

See also: 4.03 A Class Act; 6.03 Recognizing Nothingness; 6.07 Moiré Patterns; 6.09 Great Examples: 1+1=3 or more

Math Connection: Students may be familiar with tangrams (squares cut into geometric shapes that can be used to model objects). Have students create their own tangrams by cutting a square into geometric shapes for a classmate to solve or to rearrange into the shapes of various objects.

Art/Science Connection: Students can represent the interconnectedness of the parts of the natural world by creating an animal puzzle in which the shapes of the animals fit together to create the finished puzzle. Students can work with a partner or in a small group. They could begin by sketching the design (by hand or with computer software) and deciding how to make the parts, or by sketching one animal and drawing the others around it. When the puzzles are finished, have students share their results and appreciate the variety of ways in which the puzzles were made.

Science Connection: Ask students: *Describe the wholes and parts of the human physiology.* (the "wholes" of one level are the parts of another level; cells are the "wholes" of cellular biology, but parts of tissue biology, and so on) *In what ways is the whole of the human physiology greater than the sum of the parts?* You may wish to have students answer similar questions about astronomy, climate, mechanical systems, and other topics they have studied in science.

Movement Connection: Students could create a "living machine" of interconnected parts. They can figure out how each part (an individual student) will move and how the movements will connect with other movements. For example, they can stand in a line, and once the person at the end is "started" each action starts the actions of the person next in line. They could also create a more complex, non-linear machine. They might like to set their movements to music.

Art/Math/Social Studies Connection: Ask students: *What are some examples of symmetry found in nature?* (design of a leaf, snowflakes, butterfly wings). Ask students to find and share with the class symmetry patterns from the art of their own and others' cultures. Students can create their own symmetrical design based on one or more of the patterns.

Language Arts Connection: Ask students: *In a work of literature what is the whole and what are the parts?* Share the following quotation about by Ernest Hemingway about writing literature:

Any part you make will represent the whole if it is made truly.

Ask students: *What do you think this quotation means?* (a story is built on elements that reflect each other and which reflect the whole work from various angles)

See also: 6.02 Identifying Patterns

9.07 Aha!

Synopsis: Students reflect on breakthroughs in their understanding.

Ask students: *What is intuition?* (direct perception of truth without reasoning, "gut feeling") *When have you used your intuition to make a decision? What experiences have you had of ignoring your intuition, and then later realizing it was correct?*

It is always with excitement that I wake up in the morning wondering what my intuition will toss up to me, like gifts from the sea. I work with it and rely upon it. It's my partner.
Jonas Salk

*There are two ways to live your
life. One is as though nothing is a
miracle. The other is as though
everything is a miracle.*
Albert Einstein

Ask students to recall "Aha!" moments they have experienced — moments
when they glimpsed at the interconnectedness of life, had a breakthrough in a
problem they were solving, or had an insight into something they were thinking
about. Often, these moments are described as epiphanies or "light bulb"
moments, when one experiences a moment of revelation or understanding.
Students can record any "aha" moments or intuition they experience over a
week's time and then report their experiences to the class. When discussing the
experiences, ask: *How did you verify that your insight was correct?*

Science Connection: Discuss the role intuition can play in scientific
discoveries. Ask: *How can a subjective experience such as intuition be useful to an
objective activity, such as scientific research? Why would it be important to
objectively test any insights that arose from intuition or other subjective
experiences?* Discuss the following quotation by Albert Einstein:

The intellect has little to do on the road to discovery. There comes a leap in
consciousness, call it intuition or what you will, and the solution comes to
you and you don't know how or why.

Ask: *What experiences does this quotation remind you of? What is the role of
intellect once a discovery has been made through intuition?*

9.08 Ten Wonderful Things

Discuss the Einstein quotation in the margin. Ask: *What do you think Einstein
means? Which of the two ways do you tend toward in your thinking? Why?* Invite
students to share any experiences they have had or know that they might
consider to be a miracle. (Students may be more comfortable reflecting on this
topic with a journal entry.)

Ask students to create a list of "Ten Wonderful Things About My Life" in
which they can include experiences, observations, insights, ideas, or goals that
are especially important to them. Alternately, they can create a list of "Ten
Things I've Learned in My Life" to record important lessons they have learned
and advice they would pass on to others.

Extension: Discuss the following quotation:

The master views the parts with compassion, because he understands the
whole.— *Lao-tse*

Ask: *What do you think this quotation means? What experiences does it remind
you of? How might this quotation help you in your daily life?*

9.09 Great Examples: A Personal Hall of Fame

Synopsis: Students imagine conversations with great historical figures.

Ask students: *If you could speak with any historical figure from any time, whom would you choose, and why? What would you talk about?* After students have had a chance to reflect on their answers, ask for volunteers. Students may be interested to note that imagining great historical figures is a time-honored technique of gaining insight into a situation. For example when given an assignment in Language Arts, students could ask themselves, "What would William Shakespeare do when faced with this assignment?" Have students choose who they would like to have in their own personal "hall of fame" to call upon. To prompt students' thinking, ask them to consider which famous people they would like to invite to a dinner party. Encourage students to imagine conversations they would have with their guests and conversations between the guests. These conversations require empathy, a skill which may prove useful when solving problems or making decisions.

Students can complete Worksheet 9B: **My Personal Best** to summarize their own great skills and qualities.

Extension: You may want to structure a debate or conversation in which each student plays a famous person and represents that person's viewpoint.

Social Studies Connection: Have students choose a historical figure from a different cultural background than their own, and explain how the insights and understandings from that culture help to strengthen and enrich their own cultural identity.

Study the actions of illustrious men to see how they have borne themselves, examine the causes of their victories and defeats, so as to imitate the former and avoid the latter.
Niccolo Machiavelli

Supporting Learning: Encourage students to read biographies of famous people. You may wish to create a bulletin board where students can list their favorite biographies, or members of their personal halls of fame.

Supporting Learning: If students have difficulty thinking of ten things, they can use common proverbs and show how they apply to the lessons they have learned.

Name:_____

If I Were an Electron

Many important breakthroughs in science have come about because of a scientist's ability to empathize with what was being studied. Match the following scientists to their quotation. You may have to research to find the answers.

CHALLENGE QUESTION: In addition to their ability to empathize with the objects they studied, what achievement do all of these scientists have in common? Watch for the answer while you research.

QUOTATION	Scientists
1. *"I know every plant in the field. I know them intimately, and I find it a pleasure to know them."*	Richard P. Feynman
2. *"I literally had to be able to think, for example, 'What would it be like if I were one of the chemical pieces in a bacterial chromosome?' and try to understand what my environment was, try to know where I was, try to know when I was supposed to function in a certain way, and so forth."*	Jacques Monod Hannes Alfven Sir Ernest Rutherford
3. He said he had to *"identify myself with a molecule of protein."*	Barbara McClintock
4. To him, *"Atoms and alpha particles were as real... as his friends."*	Subrahmanyan Chandrasekhar Joshua Lederburg
5. He made many of his discoveries in astrophysics by imagining the universe *"from the point of view of the star."*	
6. He asked, *"If I were an electron, what would I do?"*	
7. *"Instead of treating hydromagnetic equations I prefer to sit and ride on each electron and ion and try to imagine what the world is like from its point of view and what forces push it to the left or right."*	

Name: _____

My Personal Best

Take a few minutes to consider the great things about your life. Then finish the sentences below.

1. I know I did a great thing when I ... _____
   _____
   _____

2. One great thing I'd like to do is ... _____
   _____
   _____

3. One thing great about me is ... _____
   _____
   _____

4. One great idea I have is ... _____
   _____
   _____

5. A great person I admire is _____ because _____
   _____

6. One day I would like to be able to ... _____
   _____
   _____

7. If I had enough skill I would _____
   _____
   _____

Name : _____

Self-Assessment: Synthesizing

Use the middle column to write your answers to each of the following questions. At a later date, re-assess your skill in synthesizing by completing the right hand column.

	Date:	Date:
1. When I think of *synthesizing*, I think of…		
2. Understanding how people feel helps me to…		
3. Understanding how things work helps me to…		
4. Breaking a whole into parts helps me to…		
5. Putting parts together into a whole helps me to…		
6. I think "The Whole Is Greater than the Sum of the Parts" means…		

Recommended Resources

Armstrong, Tricia. 2000. *Information Transformation*. Markham: Pembroke Publishers.

Bohm, David and F. David Peat. 1987. *Science, Order, and Creativity*. New York: Bantam Books.

Boostrom, Robert. 1994. *Developing Creative and Critical Thinking: An Integrated Approach*. Lincolnwood, IL: National Textbook Company.

Briggs, John. 1988. *Fire in the Crucible: The Alchemy of Creative Genius*. New York: St. Martin's Press.

Feynman, Richard P. 1999. *The Pleasure of Finding Things Out: The Best Short Works of Richard P. Feynman*. Cambridge: Perseus Books.

Finke, Ronald. 1990. *Creative Imagery: Discoveries and Inventions in Visualization*. Hillsdale, NJ: Lawrence Erlbaum Associates.

Foster, Graham, et al. 2002. *I Think, Therefore I Learn!* Markham, ON: Pembroke Publishers.

Gardner, Howard. 1993. *Creating Minds: An Anatomy of Creativity Seen Through the Lives of Freud, Einstein, Picasso, Stravinsky, Eliot, Graham, and Gandhi*. New York: Basic Books.

Harvey, Stephanie, and Anne Goudvis. 2000. *Strategies that Work*. Portland, ME: Stenhouse.

Koechlin, Carol and Sandi Zwaan. 2001. *InfoTasks for Successful Learning*. Markham, ON: Pembroke Publishers.

Koestler, Arthur. 1964. *The Act of Creation*. London: Arkana.

Lattimer, Heather. 2003. *Thinking Through Genre*. Portland, ME: Stenhouse.

McGrayne, Sharon Bertsch. 1993. *Nobel Prize Women in Science: Their Lives, Struggles, and Momentous Discoveries*. New York: Birch Lane Press.

McGrayne, Sharon Bertsch. 2001. *Prometheans in the Lab: Chemistry and the Making of the Modern World*. McGraw-Hill.

McMackin, Mary and Barbara Siegel. 2002. *Knowing How*. Portland, ME: Stenhouse.

Michalko, Michael. 2001. *Cracking Creativity: The Secrets of Creative Genius*. Berkeley: Ten Speed Press.

Miller, Arthur, I. 1996. *Insights of Genius: Imagery and Creativity in Science and Art*. New York: Springer-Verlag.

Morgan, Norah and Juliana Saxton. 1994. *Asking Better Questions*. Markham, ON: Pembroke Publishers.

Norman, Donald A. 1993. *Things that Make Us Smart: Defending Human Attributes in the Age of the Machine*. Reading, MA: Addison-Wesley.

Ochse, R. 1990. *Before the Gates of Excellence: The Determinants of Creative Genius*. Cambridge: Cambridge University Press.

Parlette, Snowdon. 1997. *The Brain Workout Book*. New York: M. Evans and Co.

Perkins, David. 2000. *Archimedes' Bathtub: The Art and Logic of Breakthrough Thinking*. New York: W.W. Norton & Co.

Root-Bernstein, Robert Scott. 1989. *Discovering: Inventing and Solving Problems at the Frontiers of Scientific Knowledge*. Cambridge, MA: Harvard University Press.

Root-Bernstein, Robert Scott, and Michele Root-Bernstein. 1999 *Sparks of Genius: The Thirteen Thinking Tools of the World's Most Creative People*. Boston: Houghton Mifflin. Co.

Rothenberg, Albert. 1979. *The Emerging Goddess: The Creative Process in Art, Science, and Other Fields*. Chicago: The University of Chicago Press.

Schneider, Michael S. 1994. *Beginner's Guide to Constructing the Universe: The Mathematical Archetypes of Nature, Art, and Science*. HarperCollins

Shropshire, Walter Jr., ed. 1981. *The Joys of Research* Smithsonian Institute.

Siler, Todd. 1990. *Breaking the Mind Barrier: The Artscience of Neurocosmology*. New York: Simon & Schuster.

Tahan, Malba. 1993. *The Man Who Counted: A Collection of Mathematical Adventures*. New York: W.W. Norton & Co.

von Oech, Roger. 2001. *Expect the Unexpected (or you won't find it): A Creativity Tool Based on the Ancient Wisdom of Heraclitus*. New York: Simon & Schuster, Inc.

Wujec, Tom. 1988. *Pumping Ions: Games and Exercises to Flex Your Mind*. Toronto: Doubleday.

Index